FABULOUS QUILTS *from* FAVORITE PATTERNS

from *Australian Patchwork & Quilting* Magazine

Martingale™
& COMPANY

Fabulous Quilts from Favorite Patterns: From
Australian Patchwork & Quilting Magazine
© 2003 Martingale & Company

That Patchwork Place® is an imprint
of Martingale & Company™

Martingale & Company
20205 144th Avenue NE
Woodinville, WA 98072-8478
www.martingale-pub.com

The quilt designs in this book were originally
published by Express Publications Pty., Ltd.
Photographs courtesy of Express Publications.

CREDITS

President — Nancy J. Martin

CEO — Daniel J. Martin

Publisher — Jane Hamada

Editorial Director — Mary V. Green

Managing Editor — Tina Cook

Technical Editor — Karen Costello Soltys

Copy Editor — Karen Koll

Design Director — Stan Green

Illustrator — Robin Strobel

Cover and Text Designer — Shelly Garrison

Printed in China
08 07 06 05 04 03   8 7 6 5 4 3 2 1

Library of Congress Cataloging-in-Publication Data
Fabulous quilts from favorite patterns:
from Australian Patchwork & Quilting Magazine.
    p. cm.
 ISBN 1-56477-468-6
1. Patchwork—Patterns. 2. Quilting—Patterns.
I. Australian Patchwork & Quilting Magazine.
 TT835 .F315 2003
 746.46'041—dc21

                              2002151320

MISSION STATEMENT

Dedicated to providing quality products
and service to inspire creativity.

CONTENTS

INTRODUCTION

I've been making quilts for over twenty years, and while I've taken many different classes and tried all sorts of techniques along the way, my true love of quilts remains centered in tradition. I love classic-looking patchwork and appliqué, and the scrappier the mix of fabrics the better!

That's why I just love this collection of quilts from some of Australia's top quilters. I'm sure you'll enjoy these fabulous quilts, too. Many of the patterns are steeped in tradition, yet the finished quilts offer a new twist on color, an interesting border treatment, or a shortcut technique to make the stitching a breeze.

If you love appliqué, you'll find beautiful patterns such as "Lakesview" on page 29 or "Prairie Meadow" on page 69 to inspire you to pick up your thimble. For dedicated piecers, there are intricate-looking designs, like "Scrappy Gretchen" on page 85, that are not hard to make. The quick and easy shortcut for "Scrappy Gretchen" lets you throw away the templates usually associated with this pattern. You simply rotary cut squares and triangles and you end up with a fascinating and truly scrappy block.

You'll find small quilts, like the adorable "Stars in My Garden" on page 49 that features 4" blocks and fast fusible-appliqué border accents. And there are plenty of lap-size and bed quilts, too. In short, our quiltmaking friends from Down Under have come up with so many great quilt ideas that it was a challenge to pare down the number of projects to fit them all in one book.

Whatever your fancy, I'm sure you'll find quite a few quilts in this project-packed collection that you will want to make. The only dilemma will be which one to start first!

Karen Costello Soltys

Editor

BROKEN DISHES

The Broken Dishes block is wonderfully easy to stitch and it has plenty of charm, particularly when made from a lovely selection of fabrics.

Jeanette Thompson made this appealing quilt using a variety of red and blue scraps in dark, medium, and light values. You can make your own version of this classic following a planned color scheme or one that's totally scrappy.

MATERIALS

Yardages are based on 42"-wide (107 cm) fabric.

◆ 3½ yds. (3.2 m) *total* of assorted red and blue prints for blocks (5" or 12.5 cm charm squares are suitable.)

◆ 1¼ yds. (1.2 m) of medium blue print for outer border

◆ ⅝ yd. (60 cm) of red print for inner border

◆ ½ yd. (50 cm) of light blue print for middle border

◆ ⅔ yd. (60 cm) of blue print for binding

◆ 4⅝ yds. (4.2 m) of backing fabric

◆ 80" x 80" (203 cm square) piece of batting

*Made by Jeanette Thompson,
machine quilted by Snutcat Quilting Services.*

Finished Block Size: 8" x 8" (20 cm square)
Finished Quilt Size: 73½" x 73½" (187 cm square)

CUTTING

All cutting dimensions include ¼" seam allowances. Instructions are for cutting strips across the fabric width except where noted.

From the assorted red prints, cut:
◆ 98 squares, 4⅞" x 4⅞"; crosscut diagonally to yield 196 triangles

From the assorted blue prints, cut:
◆ 98 squares, 4⅞" x 4⅞"; crosscut diagonally to yield 196 triangles

From the red print for inner border, cut:
◆ 7 strips, 2½" x 42"

From the light blue print, cut:
◆ 7 strips, 2" x 42"

From the medium blue print, cut:
◆ 8 strips, 5½" x 42"

From the blue print, cut:
◆ 7 binding strips, 3" x 42"

BLOCK ASSEMBLY

1 Sort all the triangles according to color and light, medium, and dark values. Arrange the triangles for each block as shown below. Color placement isn't critical, but value is.

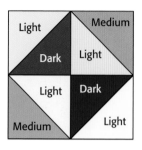

2 Chain piece the triangles together in pairs along their long sides, mixing up the prints as much as possible but keeping the values the same for each block. Press the seam allowances to one side and trim away the dog-ears at the corners of the blocks. You will then have a total of 196 triangle squares.

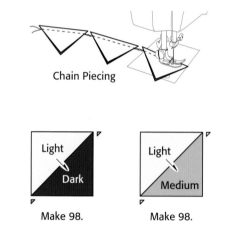

Chain Piecing

Make 98.   Make 98.

3 Sew 4 triangle squares together to complete a block. Press the seams in opposite directions. Repeat to make a total of 49 blocks.

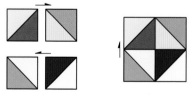

Make 49.

QUILT ASSEMBLY

1 Referring to the quilt photo opposite and the quilt assembly diagram below, arrange the blocks to make 7 rows of 7 blocks. All blocks should be positioned so that a light triangle is in the upper left corner. Balance the variety of colors and prints across the quilt top.

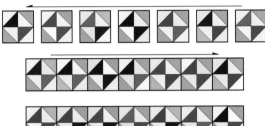

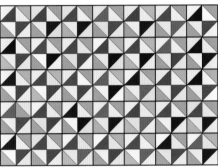

Quilt Assembly

2 Join the blocks together into rows, pressing the seams of each row in alternate directions. Join the rows together to complete the quilt top; press.

BORDERS

1 For the inner border, join the 7 red strips end to end to make 1 long strip. Press the seams open. From this length cut four 62"-long strips.

2 For the middle border, join the 7 light blue strips end to end to make 1 long strip. Press the seams open. From this length cut four 66"-long strips.

3 For the outer border, join the 8 medium blue strips end to end to make 1 long strip. Press the seams open. From this length cut four 72"-long strips.

4 The inner, middle, and outer borders are joined together before being added to the quilt top. Pin-mark the center of each strip and then join them together to make 4 sets each with a red, light blue, and medium blue strip. Press all the seams toward the outer, medium blue border.

5 Pin-mark the center of each side of the quilt top and then add the border sets, matching the centers. As you sew the borders to the quilt top, take care to begin and end stitching exactly ¼" from the corners of the quilt top; don't stitch into the seam allowances. Press the seams toward the inner border.

6 To miter the corners, lay the quilt top on an ironing board, wrong side up. Working on 1 corner at a time, fold the borders at a 45° angle, checking that the outer edges make a perfect right angle where the 2 borders meet. Press, pin, and then stitch along the 45° folds. Finally, trim the excess border fabric leaving a ¼" seam allowance. Press the seams open. Repeat for all 4 corners.

FINISHING

1 Cut the backing fabric into 2 equal lengths, remove the selvages, and join the 2 pieces together side by side to make a backing with 1 vertical seam. Press the seam to one side.

2 Layer the backing, batting, and quilt top, smoothing each layer from the center outward as you go. Baste the layers together at 4" intervals.

3 Hand or machine quilt as desired. Jeanette's quilt was hand-quilted in horizontal rows ½" apart with a cable design in the borders.

4 Remove the basting and trim the edges of the quilt, leaving ¼" of batting and backing beyond the pieced quilt top to fill the binding. Join the binding strips end to end using 45° seams; press the seams open. Attach the binding to the quilt, referring to "Binding" on page 94 for more details.

5 Label your quilt, including your name, the date, and any other relevant information.

INDIAN TRAILS

Using a host of stunning reproduction fabrics and a glorious floral border, Joy White made this quilt in a variation of a classic pattern—the Indian Trails block. She designed the quilt as a mystery quilt class sample, and the students who made this quilt along with Joy came up with some wonderful interpretations of the sample quilt. Get out your scrap bag and have fun creating your own version.

MATERIALS

Yardages are based on 42"-wide (107 cm) fabric.

- ◆ 2½ yds. (2.2 m) of floral print for outer border
- ◆ 2¼ yds. (2.1 m) of muslin for background
- ◆ 1⅝ yds. (1.5 m) of light print for sashing and inner border
- ◆ ⅓ yd. (25 cm) *each* of 20 different prints for blocks and sashing squares
- ◆ ¾ yd. (70 cm) of binding fabric
- ◆ 5¾ yds. (5.3 m) of backing fabric
- ◆ 86" x 102" (220 cm x 260 cm) piece of batting
- ◆ Template plastic
- ◆ Freezer paper or fusible web

Pieced and quilted by Joy White.

Finished Block Size: 14" x 14" (35.5 cm square)
Finished Quilt Size: 78½" x 94½" (199 cm x 240 cm)

CUTTING

All cutting dimensions include ¼" seam allowances. Instructions are for cutting strips across the fabric width unless otherwise stated. The circle appliqué pattern is on page 15. It does not include seam allowances.

From the muslin, cut:

◆ 4 strips, 7¾" x 42"; crosscut into 20 squares, 7¾" x 7¾"

◆ 15 strips, 2⅜" x 42"; crosscut into 240 squares, 2⅜" x 2⅜"

◆ 4 strips, 2" x 42"; crosscut into 80 squares, 2" x 2"

From *each* of the 20 prints, cut:

◆ 1 circle (20 total)

◆ 12 squares, 2⅜" x 2⅜" (240 total)

◆ 2 squares, 5⅜" x 5⅜"; cut each square once diagonally to yield 4 triangles (80 total)

◆ 4 rectangles, 1½" x 6½" (80 total)

◆ 4 rectangles, 1½" x 7½" (80 total)

From just 12 of the prints, cut:

◆ 1 square, 2½" x 2½" (12 total)

From the light print, cut:

◆ 16 strips, 2½" x 42"; crosscut into 31 strips, 2½" x 14½"

◆ 7 strips, 2½" x 42"

From the floral print, cut on the lengthwise grain:

◆ 4 strips, 6½" x length of fabric

From the binding fabric, cut

◆ 9 strips, 2¼" x 42"

BLOCK ASSEMBLY

This quilt has 20 blocks, and each one is assembled from four quarter units. Begin by making the various components.

Appliquéd Circles

1 Prepare the circles for your favorite method of hand or machine appliqué. You can fuse them in place and stitch around the edges by machine, needle-turn the edges by hand, or use freezer-paper appliqué. Note that the circle pattern does not include seam allowances, so you'll need to add them to your fabric for hand appliqué.

2 Lightly press the 7¾" muslin squares in half twice to mark the vertical and horizontal centerlines. Fold and finger-press the prepared fabric circles to mark their horizontal and vertical centers. Place a circle in the center of each muslin square using the guidelines to assist positioning and pin them in place. Appliqué in place.

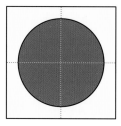

Align centers.

3 Cut each appliquéd circle block in half diagonally in both directions to yield a total of 80 triangles.

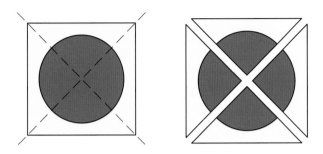

TIP — If the fabrics are a little soft or inclined to fray, use spray starch to stiffen them, but remember to wash the completed quilt. Silverfish love starch.

Triangle Squares

Using a ruler and pencil or permanent marker, draw a diagonal line on the wrong side of the 2⅜" background squares. Place each background square right sides together with a corresponding print square, and stitch ¼" away from each side of the drawn line. Cut along the drawn lines to yield 480 triangle squares, 24 of each of the prints. Press the seams toward the print triangles.

Make 24 of
each fabric
(480 total).

Quarter-Block Units

1 To assemble each quarter block, stitch a 5⅜" print triangle to a matching appliquéd triangle unit, and press the seam toward the print triangle. Repeat with the remaining 3 matching triangles and appliquéd units.

2 Stitch 6 matching triangle squares into 2 sets of 3 triangle squares each, noting that the direction of the triangles is different in each set. Add a 2½" background square to the end of one of the sets of triangle squares, as shown. Press all the seams toward the print fabrics.

3 Stitch the set of 3 triangle squares to one side of the large print triangle, making sure that the background triangles are on the outside edge, as shown. Press the seam toward the large triangle. Add the other set of triangle squares as shown.

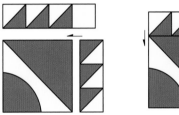

4 To complete the quarter block, add a 1½" x 6½" strip to one side of the block, so it is adjacent to the quarter circle. Then add a 1½" x 7½" strip to the adjacent side of the block as shown. For these strips, choose two different prints at random. Press both seams toward the strips.

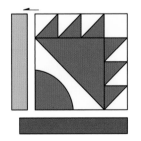 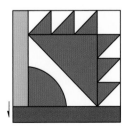

5 Join 4 quarter-block units together, turning each a quarter turn so that the long strip sides of the blocks meet in the center. Press seams to one side.

6 Repeat steps 1–5 to make 20 blocks.

QUILT ASSEMBLY

1 Arrange the 20 blocks into 5 rows, each with 4 blocks, alternating the blocks with the light print sashing strips. Sew the rows together and press the seams toward the sashing strips.

2 Make 4 sashing rows, alternating the remaining sashing strips with the sashing squares. Place the sashing rows in between the block rows, referring to the quilt photograph on page 12. Press all the seams toward the sashing strips.

3 Alternating the block and sashing rows, sew the rows together to assemble the quilt top. Pin-match each intersection carefully before stitching the rows together, then press the seams toward the sashing rows.

BORDERS

1 Join the 7 remaining 2½"-wide light print strips for the inner border into 1 long strip. Press the seams open.

2 Measure the length of the quilt top through the center; it should measure 78½". Cut 2 strips from the long light print strip to this measurement. Pin the strips to the sides of the quilt, easing to fit. Sew the borders to the quilt and press the seams toward the borders.

3 Measure the width of the quilt top through the center; it should measure 66½". Cut 2 light print strips for the top and bottom of the quilt top to this measurement. Pin them to the quilt, stitch the seams, and press the seams toward the borders.

4 For the outer border, measure the length of the quilt top again through the center; it should measure 82½". Trim 2 of the 6½"-wide outer-border strips to this measurement and stitch them to the opposite sides of the quilt top in the same manner as the first border.

5 Measure the width of the quilt top through the center; it should measure 78½". Trim the remaining 2 border strips to this measurement and add them to the top and bottom of the quilt. Press the seams toward the outer borders.

FINISHING

1 Cut the backing fabric into 2 equal lengths, remove the selvages, and join the 2 pieces side by side to make a backing with one vertical seam. Press the seam to one side.

2 Layer the backing, batting, and quilt top, smoothing each layer from the center outward as you go. Baste the layers together at 4" intervals.

3 Hand or machine quilt as desired. Joy machine quilted her quilt, stitching in the ditch around each sashing strip and horizontally and vertically across each block. She also quilted in the ditch around the block elements and stitched a curved line through each block by drawing a chalk line around a plate for a guide. The borders are quilted with a cable design.

4 Remove the basting and trim the edges of the quilt, leaving ¼" of batting and backing beyond the pieced quilt top to fill the binding. Join the nine 2"-wide binding strips end to end, using 45° seams; press the seams open. Attach the binding to the quilt, referring to "Binding" on page 94 for more details.

5 Label your quilt, including your name, the date, and any other relevant information.

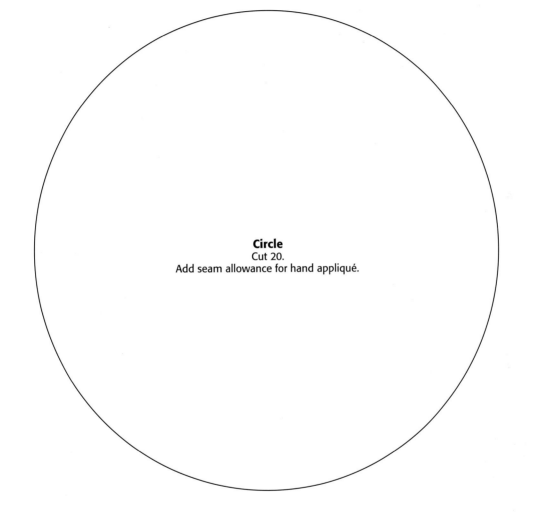

Circle
Cut 20.
Add seam allowance for hand appliqué.

NAPA VALLEY STAR

Don't be intimidated by this intricate-looking quilt. You can easily piece the Star blocks using fun shortcut techniques. And the wonderful border is foundation pieced for ease and accuracy. Tracey Browning used a charming theme fabric for her quilt, which features blue-and-white teacups, teapots, and flowers. She combined this charming chintzlike fabric pattern with matching hand-dyed blue and yellow fabrics and a white tone-on-tone print.

MATERIALS

Yardages are based on 42"-wide (107 cm) fabric.

- 3¼ yds. (3 m) of theme print for blocks, middle and pieced borders, and binding
- 1⅜ yds. (1.3 m) of medium blue mottled fabric for blocks and pieced border
- 1 yd. (90 cm) of light blue mottled fabric for sashing strips and pieced border
- ⅞ yd. (80 cm) of yellow mottled fabric for blocks and sashing squares
- ⅔ yd. (60 cm) of white-on-white print for blocks and inner border
- 4 yds. (3.7 m) of backing fabric
- 69" x 69" (175 cm square) piece of batting
- Paper for foundation piecing

Pieced and machine quilted by Tracey Browning.

Finished Block Size: 15" x 15" (38 cm square)
Finished Quilt Size: 64½" x 64½" (163 cm square)

CUTTING

All cutting dimensions include ¼" seam allowances. Instructions are for cutting strips across the fabric width.

From the yellow mottled fabric, cut:
- 3 strips, 3⅜" x 42"; crosscut into 32 squares, 3⅜" x 3⅜"
- 2 strips, 6¼" x 42"; crosscut into 8 squares, 6¼" x 6¼"
- 4 squares, 1½" x 1½"
- 2 squares, 2⅝" x 2⅝"; cut each square twice diagonally to yield 8 triangles

From the theme print, cut:
- 6 strips, 3⅜" x 42"; crosscut into 64 squares, 3⅜" x 3⅜"
- 2 strips, 6¼" x 42"; crosscut into 8 squares, 6¼" x 6¼". Then trim the remainder of the strip to 4" wide and crosscut 5 squares, 4" x 4".
- 6 strips, 3¾" x 42"
- 7 strips, 2½" x 42"

- 4 strips, 7" x 42"
- 1 strip, 2¼" x 42"; crosscut into 4 rectangles, 2¼" x 4", and 4 squares, 2¼" x 2¼"

From the medium blue mottled fabric, cut:
- 4 strips, 3" x 42"; crosscut into 48 squares, 3" x 3"
- 3 strips, 3⅜" x 42"; crosscut into 28 squares, 3⅜" x 3⅜". Cut each square once diagonally to yield 56 triangles.
- 1 strip, 3¾" x 42"; crosscut into 4 squares, 3¾" x 3¾". Cut each square twice diagonally to yield 16 triangles.
- 2 strips, 7" x 42"

From the light blue mottled fabric, cut:
- 8 strips, 1½" x 42"; crosscut into 16 strips, 1½" x 15½"
- 2 strips, 7" x 42"

From the white print, cut:
- 3 strips, 3⅜" x 42"; crosscut into 32 squares, 3⅜" x 3⅜"
- 5 strips, 1½" x 42"

TIP — As you cut the pieces, store them in labeled plastic zip-closure bags. Piecing your blocks will be much less confusing.

BLOCK ASSEMBLY

This quilt has five blocks, four half blocks, and four quarter blocks. The blocks are assembled by units, including triangle squares, flying geese, four patches, and square-in-a-square.

Triangle Squares

1 Draw a diagonal line from corner to corner on the wrong side of the 32 yellow 3⅜" squares.

2 Place each marked yellow square right sides together with a 3⅜" theme-print square. Sew a scant ¼" seam on each side of the marked lines. (These units can be chain-pieced to save time and thread if preferred.)

3 Cut along the drawn lines to yield 64 triangle squares measuring 3" x 3". Press the seam allowance toward the darker fabric.

Make 64.

Four Patches

Using 48 of the triangle squares you just made and 48 medium blue 3" squares, piece 24 four-patch units as shown. Make sure the theme-print triangles are placed toward the center of each unit.

Make 24.

Flying Geese

Use the eight 6¼" theme-print squares and the 32 white 3⅜" squares for half of the flying-geese units and the eight 6¼" yellow squares and the 32 theme-print 3⅜" squares for the other half.

1 Place two 3⅜" squares right sides together on top of a 6¼" square so the small squares are on opposite diagonal corners, as shown. Draw a line from corner to corner and stitch a scant ¼" on either side of this line. Cut along the drawn line and press the seam allowances toward the large triangles.

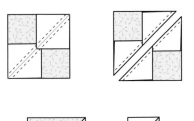

2 Place another 3⅜" square on the remaining corner of the large triangle and draw a line diagonally across the square as shown. Stitch a scant ¼" on either side of the line. Cut along the drawn line and press the triangles open to complete a flying-geese unit.

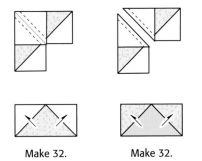

Make 32.   Make 32.

3 Repeat steps 1 and 2 with the remaining large and small squares to make 32 flying-geese units in each colorway. The units should measure 3" x 5½".

4 Sew the flying-geese units together in pairs, being careful to orient the colors as shown to make the star points for your blocks.

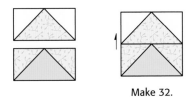

Make 32.

Square-in-a-Square Units

You need five square-in-a-square units, one for the center of each full block.

Fold a 4" theme-print square in half in each direction to mark the midpoint of each side. Fold four 3⅜" medium blue triangles in half and crease lightly to mark the midpoint of the long edges. Stitch the triangles to opposite sides of the square, matching the midpoints. Press the seams toward the triangles. Add the remaining triangles to the other two sides of the square and press them in the same manner.

Make 5.

Completing the Blocks

Each block requires 4 four-patch units, 4 flying-geese units, and 1 square-in-a-square unit. Assemble the units as shown to make a block, and then repeat to complete all 5 blocks needed.

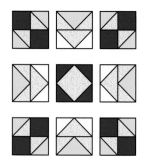 

Make 5.

HALF AND QUARTER BLOCKS

The Star blocks are set on point in this quilt, with pieced side setting and corner triangles to carry through the block design. The pieced half blocks and quarter blocks are made of three different units.

Unit 1

Sixteen of these pieced triangle units are required, two for each half block and quarter block. To make each unit 1, join two 3⅜" medium blue triangles to the theme-print sides of the remaining triangle squares made in "Triangle Squares" on page 18. Press the seams toward the blue triangles.

Unit 1
Make 16.

Unit 2

Four of these pieced triangle units are required, one for each half block. To make each unit 2, join a 3⅜" medium blue triangle to one long side of a 2¼" x 4" theme-print rectangle and press the seam toward the triangle. Join two 3¾" medium blue quarter-square triangles to the 2 short sides of the rectangle. Press the seams toward the triangles.

Unit 2
Make 4.

Unit 3

Four of these pieced triangle units are required, 1 for each quarter block. To make each unit, join the 3¾" medium blue quarter-square triangles to 2 adjacent sides of a 2¼" theme-print square. Press the seams toward the triangles.

Unit 3
Make 4.

Half-Block Assembly

Arrange a four-patch unit, two pairs of flying-geese units, two of unit 1, and one unit 2 as shown. Join the components into rows and join the rows together to form a half block. Repeat to make four half blocks.

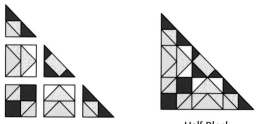

Half Block
Make 4.

Quarter-Block Assembly

Arrange a pair of flying-geese units with two of unit 1 and one unit 3 as shown. Join a unit 1 to the opposite sides of the flying-geese unit and press the seams toward unit 1. Add the unit 3 to the corner of the flying-geese units and press.

Quarter Block
Make 4.

QUILT ASSEMBLY

1 Following the quilt assembly diagram, arrange the blocks, half blocks, and quarter blocks into diagonal rows, separating them with the sashing strips, squares, and triangles.

2 Join the diagonal rows of blocks and sashing strips, squares, and triangles. Press the seams toward the sashing strips.

3 Join the rows together to form the center of the quilt top.

Quilt Assembly

BORDERS

This quilt has three borders. The inner and middle borders are plain, and the outer border is foundation pieced.

Inner Border

1 Join the five 1½"-wide white border strips together end to end and press the seams open. Measure the length of the quilt top through the center and cut 2 strips to this measurement. Sew the border strips to opposite sides of the quilt top, matching the centers and ends. Press the seams toward the borders.

2 Measure the width of the quilt top through the center, including the borders you've just added. Cut 2 strips to this measurement from the white pieced strip. Join these borders to the top and bottom of the quilt in the same manner as the side borders.

Middle Border

1 Join the six 3¾"-wide theme-print strips together end to end and press the seams open. Measure and trim 2 border strips for the sides of the quilt. Attach the strips to opposite sides of the quilt. Press the seams outward.

2 Measure the width of the quilt, including the theme-print borders you just added. Cut 2 more border strips to this length and join them to the quilt top in the same manner as for the side borders.

Outer Pieced Border

1 Cut four lengths of paper, 5½" x 58", joining the paper if necessary. The paper strips are cut a little longer than required.

2 Using your rotary-cutting ruler as a guide, draw a ¼" seam allowance line along each long edge of the paper strips, making the finished width of the third border 5".

3 Beginning approximately 2" from one end of a paper strip, measure and mark off 3" increments along the seam line. You'll need 18 segments. This is the inner edge of the border.

4 The outer edge of the foundation is also marked in 3" increments that fall at the midpoint of the segments on the inner edge, as shown below.

Mark the center point of an inner edge division and then mark the outer line directly opposite this point. Measure and mark 3" from this point, creating 19 segments on the outer seam line.

5 Draw lines across the foundation, connecting the marked points to form triangles. Then draw a ¼" seam allowance at each end of the foundation paper, to the outside of each end triangle.

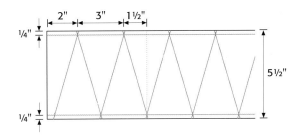

6 Repeat steps 1–5 to make 4 identical border foundation papers.

7 The pattern for the corner foundations is on page 23. Trace the pattern to make 4 corner foundations.

TIP — Paper piecing triangles can be a little tricky at first until you're familiar with placing the fabrics correctly so that they'll cover the intended part of the foundation after the seam is sewn and the patch is opened up. Here's a suggestion for cutting the pieces you'll need so they'll be large enough to cover the patches without creating excessive waste.

Make a paper template of the border triangle, adding ¼" seam allowances. Tape the template to a rotary-cutting ruler. Layer the 7"-wide strips of fabric one on top of the other to cut the pieces required for the foundation piecing. Using a rotary cutter and ruler, cut the triangles using the template as a guide.

8 To make the strips of border triangles, use the theme-print, medium blue, and light blue 7"-wide strips. Alternate the theme-print triangles with the medium and light blue triangles. The yellow theme fabric is always positioned on the outer edge of the border and the blue triangles are on the inner edge. To prevent mixing up the fabrics, you may want to mark the individual triangles on the paper with a *B* for blue and a *T* for theme print.

9 Place 1 theme-print and 1 blue triangle, right sides together and with the marked side of the foundation paper up, under the paper beneath the first marked triangle. The theme print should be against the foundation. Stitch along the marked line between the first and second triangle. Stitch at least 2 machine stitches on either side of the outer seam allowance. Trim the seam allowance and press the pieces open, ensuring the fabric covers the marked area.

10 Then, using the fabrics alternately, continue in this manner, ensuring that you're stitching each newly added triangle right side up. When each strip is completed, press and trim the strip along the outer edge of the seam allowances. *Do not trim away the seam allowances.*

11 From the fabrics remaining, cut pieces from the theme print and the blue fabrics to cover the triangle areas on the corner foundations and stitch them in the same manner. Again, the blue triangles are placed along the inner edge of the border and the theme-print triangles are placed along the outer edge. Trim around the outer edge, making sure to leave the seam allowance intact.

12 Leave the foundation papers on the borders until they have been joined to the quilt top to stabilize any stretch in the borders and create perfect points. Join 2 of the borders to the opposite sides of the quilt top. Press the seams toward the middle border.

13 Join a corner section to each end of the 2 remaining borders, taking care that they are placed in the correct direction (all blue edges along the inner edge of the border). Join the borders to the top and bottom of the quilt, pivoting the seams slightly to set-in the corner sections.

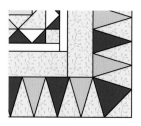

Border Corner

14 To keep the edge from stretching, stay stitch around the outer edge of the quilt top just inside the seam allowance before removing the paper foundations.

FINISHING

1 Cut the backing fabric into 2 equal lengths. Cut 1 of the pieces in half lengthwise. Remove the selvages and stitch a narrow strip to opposite sides of the full-width piece to make a backing with 2 vertical seams. Press the seams open.

2 Layer the backing, batting, and quilt top, smoothing each layer from the center outward as you go. Baste the layers together at 4" intervals.

3 Hand or machine quilt as desired. Tracey's quilt was machine quilted in the ditch around all the sashing strips. The remainder of the quilt center, except for the stars created by the white triangles, was stipple quilted with monofilament in the top

of the machine and cotton thread to match the backing in the bobbin. The inner and middle borders were both quilted in the ditch. The outer border was quilted in the ditch around the triangles.

4 Remove the basting and trim the edges of the quilt, leaving ¼" of batting and backing beyond the pieced quilt top to fill the binding. Join the 2½"-wide theme-print binding strips end to end; press the seams open. Attach the binding to the quilt, referring to "Binding" on page 94 for more details.

5 Label your quilt, including your name, the date, and any other relevant information.

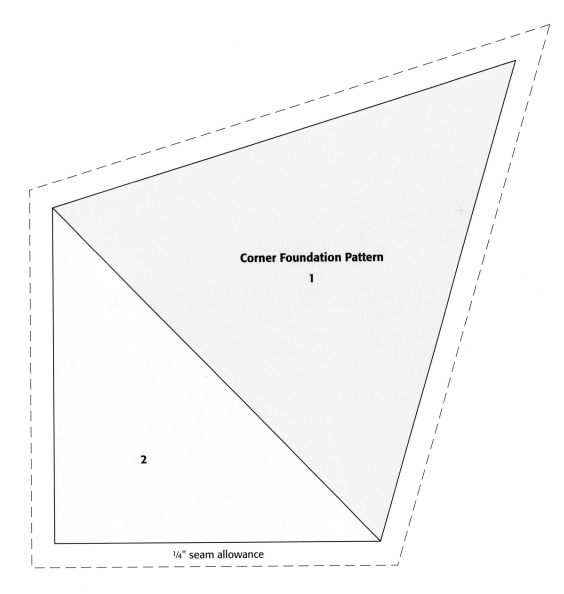

Corner Foundation Pattern

1

2

¼" seam allowance

STRIPPY FOUR PATCH

Brigitte Giblin makes quilts to be used and loved, which is precisely what should be done with this wonderful scrap quilt. Strippy Four Patch has a warm, old-fashioned feel achieved through Brigitte's use of yellows and natural tones as well as the simple Four Patch blocks that she set on point between strips of color. The polka-dot background fabric adds a touch of whimsy. This quilt will make a lovely addition to any country-style decor.

MATERIALS

Yardages are based on 42"-wide (107 cm) fabric.

- 2¼ yds. (2.1 m) of striped fabric for vertical sashing and borders
- 1⅔ yds. (1.5 m) of yellow print for setting triangles and vertical sashing
- 1⅓ yds. (1.2 m) of white with black polka dots for background
- ⅔ yd. (60 cm) *total* of assorted light fabrics for blocks and borders
- ⅔ yd. (60 cm) *total* of assorted dark fabrics for blocks and borders
- 4 yds. (3.6 m) of backing fabric
- ¾ yd. (70 cm) of red striped fabric for binding
- 70" x 80" (178 cm x 203 cm) piece of batting

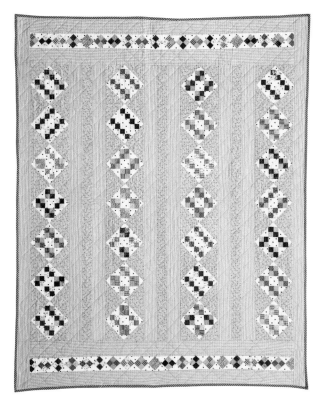

Pieced and hand quilted by Brigitte Giblin.

Finished Block Size: 5½" x 5½" (14 cm square)
Finished Quilt Size: 63⅛" x 74½" (160 cm x 189 cm)

CUTTING

All cutting dimensions include ¼" seam allowances.
Instructions are for cutting strips across the fabric
width except where noted.

From the assorted light fabrics, cut:
◆ 9 strips, 1½" x 42"

From the assorted dark fabrics, cut:
◆ 9 strips, 1½" x 42"

**From the width of the white fabric with black
polka dots, cut:**
◆ 2 strips, 2½" x 42"; crosscut into 28 squares,
2½" x 2½"

◆ 6 strips, 4⅛" x 42"; crosscut into 47 squares,
4⅛" x 4⅛". Cut squares in half diagonally in both
directions to yield 188 triangles.

◆ 4 strips, 2⅜" x 42"; crosscut into 60 squares,
2⅜" x 2⅜". Cut squares in half diagonally in one
direction to yield 120 triangles.

**From the yellow print, cut on the lengthwise
grain:**
◆ 3 strips, 3" x length of fabric

From the remaining yellow print, cut:
◆ 12 squares, 9" x 9"; cut the squares in half
diagonally in both directions to yield 48 triangles

◆ 8 squares, 4⅞" x 4⅞"; cut the squares in half
diagonally in one direction to yield 16 triangles

**From the striped fabric, cut on the lengthwise
grain:**
◆ 8 strips, 3½" x length of fabric

◆ 4 strips, 4" x length of fabric

From the red striped fabric, cut:
◆ 3"-wide bias strips, enough to yield 290" of
binding

BLOCK ASSEMBLY

1 Stitch the 1½"-wide light and dark strips together
in pairs. Press the seam allowances toward the
dark strips. Crosscut the strip sets into 1½"-wide
segments. You'll need a total of 304 segments.

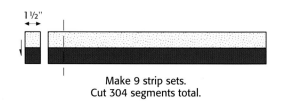

Make 9 strip sets.
Cut 304 segments total.

2 Sew the segments together to create 152 four-
patch units with the dark fabrics diagonally
opposite each other. You'll need 112 four-patch
units for the quilt blocks; reserve the remaining
40 units for the top and bottom borders.

3 To assemble the block, arrange 4 four-patch units,
one 2½" polka-dot square, four 2⅜" polka-dot
triangles, and four 4⅛" polka-dot triangles as
shown. Sew the squares and triangles together in
diagonal rows, adding the quarter-square triangles
last. Press the block; then trim it to 6" square.
Repeat to make a total of 28 blocks.

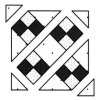

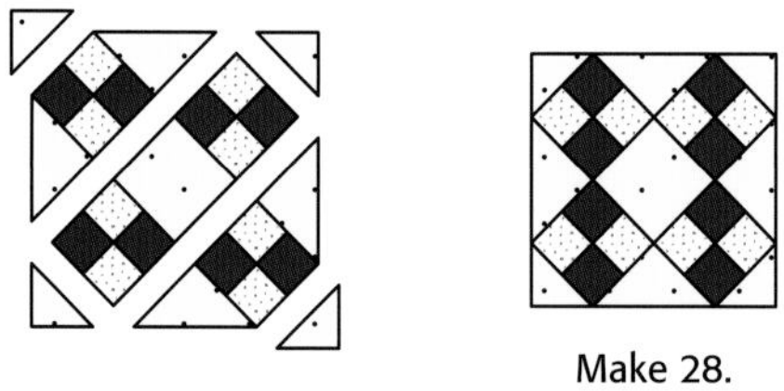

Make 28.

QUILT ASSEMBLY

The quilt is assembled in strips. There are four strips of blocks, each with seven blocks. These strips are separated by long strips of striped and yellow fabric.

1 Stitch 9" yellow setting triangles to opposite sides of 20 of the Four Patch blocks as shown and press the seams toward the triangles.

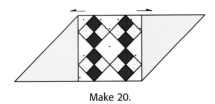

Make 20.

2 To make the 8 end units, add a 9" yellow setting triangle to 1 side and yellow corner triangles to 2 sides as shown. Press the seams toward the triangles.

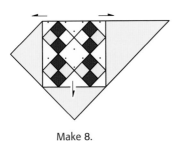

Make 8.

3 Join 5 block units and 2 end units together as shown to make each block row.

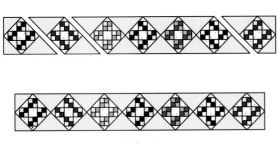

Make 4.

4 To make the 3 vertical sashing rows, stitch the 3½" striped strips to either side of the 3" yellow strips and press the seams toward the striped fabric.

5 Sew the rows of blocks and the sashing strips together. Press the seams toward the sashing.

BORDERS

1 Using the remaining four-patch units from step 2 of "Block Assembly" opposite, stitch 4⅛" polka-dot setting triangles to the opposite sides of 36 of the units as shown. Press the seams toward the triangles. For the 4 end units add a 4⅛" setting triangle to one side and 2⅜" corner setting triangles to 2 sides. Press the seams toward the triangles.

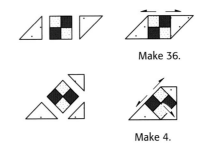

Make 36.

Make 4.

2 Join the units together to make 2 border strips with 18 block units and 2 end units per border. Trim 4"-wide striped border strip to the length of your quilt (approximately 57") and sew to either side of each pieced border strip; then join them to the top and bottom of the quilt. Press.

3 Measure the length of the quilt top through the center and trim the remaining striped border strips to this length. Sew the borders to the sides of the quilt and press.

FINISHING

1 Cut the backing fabric into 2 equal lengths, remove the selvages, and join the 2 pieces together side by side to make a backing with 1 horizontal seam. Press the seam to one side.

2 Layer the backing, batting, and quilt top, and baste the layers together at 4" intervals.

3 Hand or machine quilt as desired. Brigitte hand quilted a 2" diagonal grid over the entire surface.

4 Remove the basting and trim the edges of the quilt, leaving ¼" of batting and backing beyond the pieced quilt top to fill the binding. Join the 3"-wide bias strips end to end for binding; press the seams open. Attach the binding to the quilt, referring to "Binding" on page 94 for more details.

5 Label your quilt, including your name, the date, and any other relevant information.

LAKESVIEW

Michelle Marvig's stunning quilt combines Tree Everlasting patchwork panels with fusible appliqué panels and an unusual scalloped border. Notice how the scallops face toward the center of the quilt rather than toward the outer edges. Michelle used reproduction fabrics that consist of pretty floral designs with dark olive, green, pink, and blue as the prominent colors. For a similar look, you can substitute any reproduction fabrics. Or choose a more contemporary color palette all your own. Either way, the eye-catching blend of easy piecing and appliqué makes this quilt a must to sew.

MATERIALS

Yardages are based on 42"-wide (107 cm) fabric.

◆ 2⅛ yds. (1.9 m) of large floral print for border

◆ 16 fat eighths of assorted dark prints for patchwork panels, including pinks, greens, blues, blacks, and burgundies

◆ 1⅔ yds. (1.4 m) of beige stripe for appliqué panels

◆ 10 fat eighths of assorted light prints for patchwork panels

◆ ½ yd. (50 cm) of green stripe fabric for vine and stems

◆ ⅝ yd. (50 cm) of dark green print for binding

◆ 4¼ yds. (3.8 m) of backing fabric

◆ 75" x 75" (190 cm square) piece of batting

◆ Fusible web

◆ Template plastic

◆ Rayon threads for machine appliqué

Pieced, machine appliquéd, and machine quilted by Michelle Marvig.

Finished Quilt Size: 66½" x 67½"
(169 cm x 171.5 cm)

CUTTING

All cutting dimensions include ¼" seam allowances. Instructions are for cutting strips across the fabric width except where noted.

From *each* of the 16 dark prints, cut:

◆ 1 strip, 2⅞" x 20"; crosscut into 5 squares, 2⅞" x 2⅞". Cut the squares once diagonally to yield 160 half-square triangles.

From the balance of each strip, cut:

◆ 2 squares, 2½" x 2½"

◆ 1 strip, 2½" x 20"; crosscut into 8 squares, 2½" x 2½". (This makes a total of ten 2½" squares from each dark fabric.)

From *each* of the 10 light prints, cut:

◆ 2 strips, 2⅞" x 20"; crosscut into 8 squares, 2⅞" x 2⅞". Cut the squares once diagonally to yield 160 half-square triangles.

From the beige stripe fabric, cut on the lengthwise grain:

◆ 2 strips, 9½" x 52"

◆ 2 strips, 5" x 52"

From the large floral print, cut on the lengthwise grain:

◆ 2 strips, 8½" x 70"

◆ 2 strips, 8½" x 52"

◆ 2 strips, 3" x 52"

From the dark green print, cut:

◆ 7 strips, 2½" x 42"

PATCHWORK PANELS

1 Sew the 2⅞" dark and light triangles together in pairs to make 160 triangle squares. (You'll need only 150, but the extra triangle squares will give you more choices when you lay out the "trees.") Mix up the fabric combinations to keep things interesting. Press the seams toward the dark triangles.

Make 160.

2 Each of the 3 panels is made of 25 patchwork rows. Each row consists of two 2½" dark squares in the middle and a triangle square on each end. Lay out the pieces for 1 panel at a time on your design wall or table.

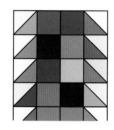

Join 25 rows to make 1 panel. Make 3 panels.

3 Sew the squares and triangle squares together 1 row at a time. Press the seams in each row in alternating directions. Sew the rows together to make the panel and press the seams toward the bottom of the row.

4 Repeat to make a total of 3 patchwork panels.

APPLIQUÉ PANELS

Both the floral appliqué panels and the scalloped edges on Michelle's quilt were done with fusible appliqué that was machine blanket stitched with matching rayon threads. If you prefer, you can do the appliqué by hand. The patterns for the appliqué are on page 33.

1 Measure the length of all the patchwork panels. They should be 50½" long. Trim the two 9½"-wide beige strips to this length.

2 Iron fusible web to the wrong side of the ½ yard of green stripe fabric. Do not peel off the backing paper. Place the 45° line of your ruler along the bottom edge of the fabric with the angled edge of the ruler passing through the corner of the fabric. Cut along the angled edge of the ruler. Slide your ruler along the fabric to cut six ½"-wide strips parallel to this line for the vines.

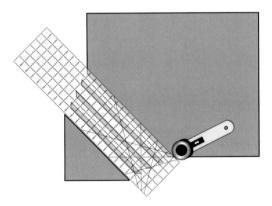

3 Prepare plastic templates for the flower stems and vine ends. Trace 5 stems, 5 reversed stems, and 4 vine ends onto the remaining green fabric already prepared with fusible web.

4 For the remaining appliqué pieces, trace 10 flowers, 4 buds, and 23 leaves onto the paper side of the fusible web. Cut the shapes out roughly, fuse the flower and bud shapes to the wrong side of the pink fabrics left over from the patchwork panels, and cut them out carefully on the drawn lines. Fuse the leaves to the wrong side of the leftover green fabrics and cut them out on the line.

5 Refer to the quilt photograph opposite to assist you with the placement of the vines. Peel off the paper backing and curve a length of bias on the background and pin it in place when you're satisfied with its placement. Slip the flower stems and leaves under the vine and pin them in place. Slip the flowers and buds under the ends of the stems. Place a new section of vine under the end of the piece already in place. When you are satisfied with the placement of the vines, leaves, and flowers, fuse them in place. Repeat to make the second panel, positioning the vine so it is a mirror image of the vine on the first panel.

6 Stitch around all the raw edges of the appliqué shapes using a machine blanket stitch and matching rayon threads.

SCALLOPED PANELS

1 Trace 20 scallops onto the paper side of fusible web and cut them out. Cut the 5"-wide beige strips to the same length as the vine panels— 50½" or whatever your quilt length is. Trim the two 3"-wide floral strips to this length, too.

2 Leaving a ¼" seam allowance on both ends of the floral fabric strip, place 10 of the fusible web scallops on the wrong side of the floral strip, spacing them evenly. They can then be trimmed if necessary. Fuse the scallops in place; then cut out the long strip of scallops and fuse it along 1 edge of the 5"-wide beige strip. Blanket stitch around the raw edge of the scallops.

Fuse scallops to bottom edge of beige strip.
Blanket stitch around edges.

3 Repeat to make a second panel in the same manner.

QUILT ASSEMBLY

1 Sew a vine appliqué panel to each side of a Tree Everlasting patchwork panel. Press the seams toward the vine panels.

2 Sew the remaining patchwork panels to the outer edges of the vine panels. Make sure the direction of the outer patchwork panels is the same as that of the center patchwork panel. Press the seams toward the vine panels.

3 Complete the center of the quilt by adding the scalloped panels to the edges of the patchwork panels so the scallops are on the outer edges. Press the seams toward the scalloped panels.

BORDER

1 Measure the width of your quilt through the center; it should be approximately 50½" wide. Trim the 8½" x 55" floral border strips to this measurement and sew them to the top and bottom of the quilt. Press the seams toward the borders.

2 Measure the length of the quilt through the center; it should be approximately 67½" long. Trim the remaining 2 floral border strips to this measurement and sew them to the opposite sides of the quilt. Press the seams toward the borders.

FINISHING

1 Layer the backing, batting, and quilt top, smoothing each layer from the center outward as you go. Baste the layers together at 4" intervals.

2 Hand or machine quilt as desired. Michelle machine quilted in the ditch of the panels as well as around the scallops and the appliqué shapes. The squares in the middle of the patchwork panels are quilted with triangles to add more texture. The background of the vine panels is free-motion quilted with tendrils curling from the vine. The beige area around the scallops is quilted with spiral meandering.

3 Remove the basting and trim the edges of the quilt, leaving ¼" of batting and backing beyond the pieced quilt top to fill the binding. Join the 2½"-wide binding strips end to end; press the seams open. Attach the binding to the quilt, referring to "Binding" on page 94 for more details.

4 Label your quilt, including your name, the date, and any other relevant information.

Quilt Assembly

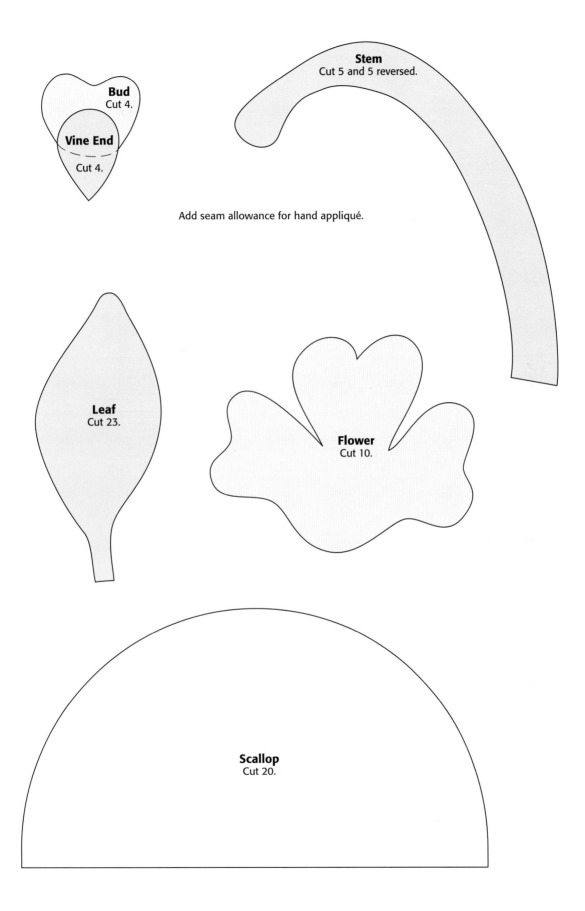

Bud
Cut 4.

Vine End
Cut 4.

Stem
Cut 5 and 5 reversed.

Add seam allowance for hand appliqué.

Leaf
Cut 23.

Flower
Cut 10.

Scallop
Cut 20.

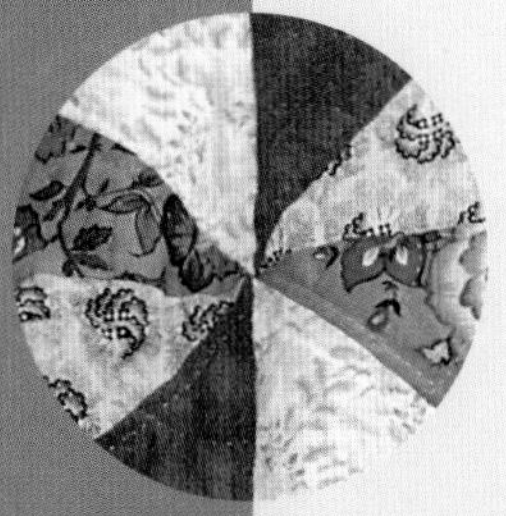

PIE QUILT

This original, scrappy quilt is a delightful way to showcase a special collection of fabrics, such as the reproduction fabrics Brigitte Giblin has used. The curved seams are gentle enough to ease, just as with a Drunkard's Path block, but the effect is strikingly different. The "pie slices" are assembled into blocks that Brigitte assures are as easy as pie to make.

To make the color placement a snap, simply number your fabrics and follow the chart to create a truly wonderful quilt.

MATERIALS

Yardages are based on 42"-wide (107 cm) fabric.

- 12 fat quarters or scraps of assorted light prints for Pie blocks

- 1⅝ yds. (1.5 m) of border-print fabric with a 7"-wide pattern with four repeats

- 6 fat quarters or scraps of assorted cool-tone prints—greens, blues, and mauves—for Pie blocks

- 6 fat quarters or scraps of assorted warm-tone prints—reds, burgundies, pinks, and oranges—for Pie blocks

- ⅞ yd. (80 cm) of light print or solid cream for background

- ⅝ yd. (50 cm) of binding fabric

- 2½ yds. (2.3 m) of backing fabric

- 59" x 59" (150 cm square) piece of batting

- Template plastic

- Fine-point permanent marker

Machine pieced and hand quilted by Brigitte Giblin.

Finished Block Size: 9⅛" x 9⅛" (23 cm square)
Finished Quilt Size: 52¼" x 52¼" (133 cm square)

MAKING TEMPLATES

Patterns for pieces A, B, and C are on pages 38–39. If you prefer to hand piece your quilt, trace the inside seam line on your template plastic using the fine-point permanent marker and cut out. Trace around the templates onto the wrong side of your fabrics and cut out the pieces, leaving a ¼" seam allowance outside the marked line.

For machine piecing, trace the outer cutting line onto your template plastic. Cut out the plastic on the drawn line, and trace around the templates onto your fabric. Cut out the fabric pieces on the marked line; pieces will include an exact ¼" seam allowance.

CUTTING

All cutting dimensions include ¼" seam allowances. Instructions are for cutting strips across the fabric width except where noted.

From *each* of the 6 warm- and 6 cool-tone fabrics, cut:

◆ 6 of piece A

From *each* of the light print fat quarters, cut:
◆ 6 of piece A

From the light print background fabric, cut:
◆ 12 of piece C
◆ 12 of piece B

From the length of the border fabric, cut:
◆ 4 strips, 7" x the length of the fabric

From the binding fabric, cut:
◆ 6 strips, 3" x 42"

TIP — To plan a quilt like that pictured, number your fabrics and follow the quilt assembly diagram for fabric placement. If you are using assorted scraps you may prefer to design your own color layout.

◆ Number the cool-tone prints C1–C6
◆ Number the warm-tone prints W1–W6
◆ Number the light prints L1–L12

To keep track of your fabrics, cut a scrap of each one, paste them to a sheet of paper, and label them.

BLOCK ASSEMBLY

The quilt is made of 12 blocks and 12 half blocks. Each block has four pairs of pie segments.

1 Match the warm- and cool-tone pieces with their corresponding light prints and sew them together in pairs as indicated below. Reserve the remaining pieces for the half blocks.

6 pairs L1 + C1	4 pairs L7 + W1
4 pairs L2 + C2	6 pairs L8 + W2
6 pairs L3 + C3	4 pairs L9 + W3
4 pairs L4 + C4	6 pairs L10 + W4
6 pairs L5 + C5	4 pairs L11 + W5
4 pairs L6 + C6	6 pairs L12 + W6

2 Referring to the quilt assembly diagram for color placement, arrange 4 of the pie corner segments from step 1 around the background B piece. Finger-press or pin-mark the center of each side of the B piece. Working with the background

fabric on top, pin through the middle of the B piece so it aligns with the seam of the A pieces. Ease the edges to align the pieces along the curve, pinning as you go.

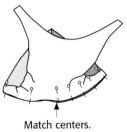

Match centers.
Pin, easing edges.

3 Sew all 4 corner segments to the background fabric to complete a block. Press the seams toward the corners.

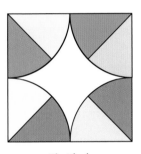

Pie Block

4 Repeat to make 2 of each of the 6 color combinations.

5 Make the 12 half blocks using the remainder of the pie corner segments, the single pie wedges, and the background C pieces. Mark the center of the long side of a C background piece, then place it on top of the pie corner segment, matching the centers. Pin and stitch the sections together.

6 Add the single pie wedges to the short sides of the C background, referring to the quilt assembly diagram below for color placement. Carefully press the seams toward the pie segments.

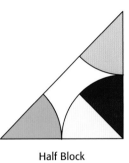

Half Block

QUILT ASSEMBLY

1 Referring to the quilt assembly diagram for the correct placement of the blocks and half blocks, arrange the blocks on your design wall or floor.

2 Sew the blocks together in diagonal rows as shown, and then sew the rows together to complete the center of the quilt.

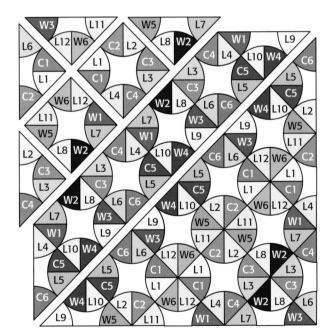

Quilt Assembly

37

BORDER

The border strips are cut longer than the length of the quilt sides so that you'll have enough fabric for mitered corners.

1 Pin-mark the center of each border and also the sides of the quilt top. Join the border strips to each side of the quilt top, matching the centers. Begin and end stitching exactly ¼" in from the corners of the quilt top. Do not trim off the extra border fabric.

2 Working on 1 corner at a time, lay out the quilt top on the ironing board, wrong side up. Fold the borders at a 45° angle at the corner, checking that the outer edges make a perfect right angle. Lightly press the angle folds, then pin and stitch the borders together along the fold lines.

3 Press the seams open and trim the excess border fabric. Complete the remaining corners in the same manner.

FINISHING

1 Trim the selvages from the sides of the backing fabric. From the 2½-yard length of backing fabric, cut a 30" piece and then cut this piece in half lengthwise, yielding 2 strips approximately 30" x 21". Sew the 2 pieces together along the shorter edges to make a 60" x 21" strip. Sew this strip to the remaining 60" length of backing fabric to complete the backing.

2 Layer the backing, batting, and quilt top, smoothing each layer from the center outward as you go. Baste the layers together at 4" intervals.

3 Hand or machine quilt as desired. Brigitte's quilt is hand quilted. There are 3 concentric circles of quilting within each pie. The first circle has a radius of 1¼", the second has a radius of 2½", and the third circle is ½" inside the outer edge of the pie. The center of each block has a 2 rows of echo quilting. The border motifs are also outline quilted.

4 Remove the basting and trim the edges of the quilt, leaving ¼" of batting and backing beyond the pieced quilt top to fill the binding. Join the 3"-wide binding strips, end to end; press the seams open. Attach the binding to the quilt, referring to "Binding" on page 94 for more details.

5 Label your quilt, including your name, the date, and any other relevant information.

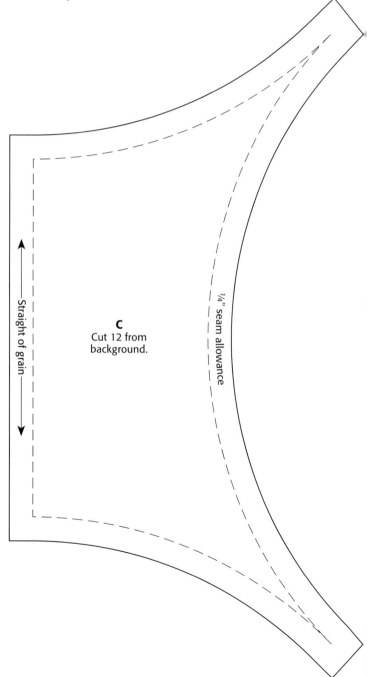

Straight of grain

C
Cut 12 from background.

¼" seam allowance

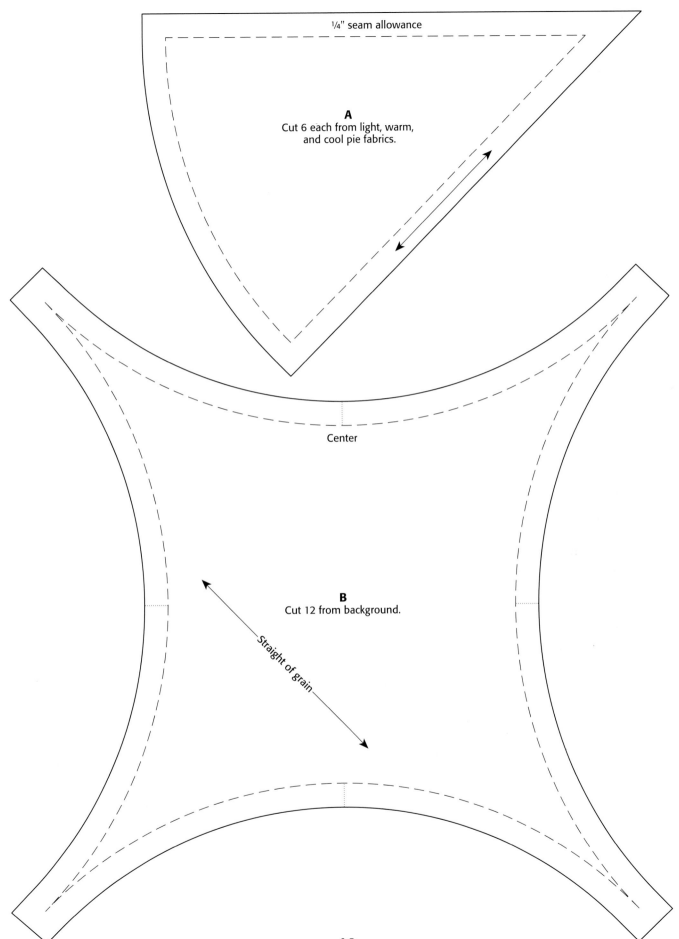

¼" seam allowance

A
Cut 6 each from light, warm,
and cool pie fabrics.

Center

B
Cut 12 from background.

Straight of grain

RED HOUSES

The charming Schoolhouse block is perfect for a friendship quilt, conjuring up images of warm hearts and warm homes. It also makes for an imaginative scrap quilt. If you have a lot of scraps in one color scheme, use them to make the positive-negative effect Diane Flindell created in her "Red Houses" quilt. Diane's friends hand and machine pieced many of the red Schoolhouse blocks, and after she received them all, Diane made the reverse alternate blocks—white houses on red backgrounds—that give this quilt its eye-catching appeal.

MATERIALS

Yardages are based on 42"-wide (107 cm) fabric.

- 5½ yds. (5 m) of cream solid for borders and block background
- ⅓ yd. (30 cm) or fat quarter of 13 different burgundy prints for borders and blocks
- 8 yds. (7.1 m) of backing fabric
- ¾ yd. (70 cm) of burgundy fabric for binding
- 94" x 94" (240 cm square) of batting
- Template plastic
- Fine-point permanent marker

Hand and machine pieced by Diane Flindell and her quilt group, the St. Ives Quilters. Machine quilted by Michelle Breeze of Licorice Lane Designs.

Finished Block Size: 12" x 12" (30.5 cm square)
Finished Quilt Size: 84½" x 84½" (215 cm square)

Cutting

All cutting dimensions include ¼" seam allowances. Instructions are for cutting strips across the fabric width except where noted. To help you keep your pieces organized, the cutting is given first for the borders, then for the red houses, and finally for the white houses. Patterns for the D, D reverse, E, F, and G templates are on pages 46–47.

Borders
From the cream fabric, cut:
- 5 strips, 3⅞" x 42"; crosscut into 44 squares, 3⅞" x 3⅞"
- From the remainder of the last strip, cut 4 squares, 3½" x 3½"

From the remaining cream fabric, cut on the lengthwise grain:
- 4 strips, 6½" x 90"
- 4 strips, 3½" x 70"

From *each* of the burgundy prints, cut:
- 4 squares, 3⅞" x 3⅞" (You'll have 52 squares; only 44 will be needed.)

From the burgundy binding fabric, cut:
- 10 strips, 2¼" x 42"

Red Houses with White Backgronds
From *each* of the 13 burgundy prints, cut:
- 2 B pieces, 1½" x 2½"
- 1 H piece, 2½" x 5½"
- 2 I pieces, 2" x 5"
- 1 L piece, 2" x 3½"
- 2 N pieces, 1¾" x 4½"
- 2 O pieces, 1½" x 6"
- 1 E piece
- 1 G piece

From the cream fabric, cut:
- 26 A pieces, 2½" x 3"
- 13 C pieces, 2½" x 5½"
- 13 J pieces, 2½" x 5"
- 13 K pieces, 1½" x 7"
- 26 M pieces, 1¾" x 3½"
- 13 P pieces, 1½" x 6½"
- 13 D pieces
- 13 D reverse pieces
- 13 F pieces

White Houses with Red Backgronds
From the cream fabric, cut:
- 24 B pieces, 1½" x 2½"
- 12 H pieces, 2½" x 5½"
- 24 I pieces, 2" x 5"
- 12 L pieces, 2" x 3½"
- 24 N pieces, 1¾" x 4½"
- 24 O pieces, 1½" x 6"
- 12 E pieces
- 12 G pieces

From *each* of the burgundy fabrics, cut:
- 2 A pieces, 2½" x 3"
- 1 C piece, 2½" x 5½"
- 1 J piece, 2½" x 5"

- ◆ 1 K piece, 1½" x 7"
- ◆ 2 M pieces, 1¾" x 3½"
- ◆ 1 P piece, 1½" x 6½"
- ◆ 1 D piece
- ◆ 1 D reverse piece
- ◆ 1 F piece

BLOCK ASSEMBLY

This quilt contains 25 Schoolhouse blocks: 13 red houses and 12 white houses. Each block is constructed in four sections. To avoid confusion or mixing up pieces, it's easiest to piece one block at a time. Following the block diagrams, arrange the pieces required for one block at a time on your sewing table or design wall. Always press the seams toward the burgundy fabric.

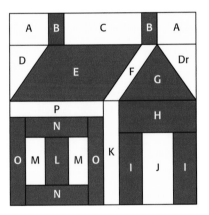

Red House

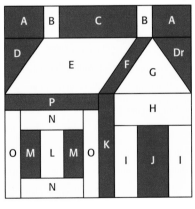

White House

1 For section 1, the chimney and sky row, sew 2 sets of A and B together, and then join them to either side of C as shown.

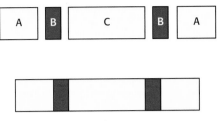

Section 1

2 For section 2, the roof row, stitch the D, E, F, G, and D reverse pieces together in a horizontal row. Take care to match the seam intersections on the angled pieces so the finished row is even.

Section 2

3 For section 3, the door unit, stitch an I piece to both long sides of a J piece. Add an H piece to the top edge and press. Stitch a K piece to the left-hand edge of the unit to complete the door section.

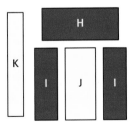
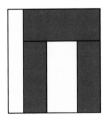

Section 3

4 For section 4, the window unit, stitch an M piece to both long sides of an L piece. Add an N piece to both the top and bottom edges of the window unit. Press. Add the O pieces to the opposite sides of the windows, and then add the P strip to the top edge of the unit. Press.

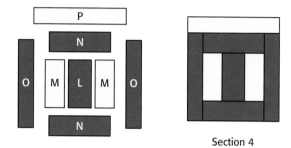

Section 4

5 Join section 3 to the right of section 4. Then stitch section 2 to the top of the windows and door, followed by section 1 stitched to the top of the roof. Carefully align seam allowances as you sew.

Repeat to make a total of 13 red houses and 12 white houses. For the red houses, press the seams between sections toward the roof section; for the white houses, press them away from the roof section. This will ensure that seams are facing in opposite directions when you join the blocks.

QUILT ASSEMBLY

The quilt is constructed in five rows of five Schoolhouse blocks each, and the red and white blocks are alternated throughout the quilt.

Referring to the photograph of the quilt on page 42, start the first row with a red block and alternate with white and red blocks across the row.

Start the second row with a white block and continue, alternating the blocks. Press the seams for each row in opposite directions so that the seams oppose when the rows are stitched together to form the center of the quilt.

BORDERS

The quilt has white inner and outer borders, separated by a red-and-white pieced sawtooth border.

Inner Border

1 Measure the width of your quilt; it should measure approximately 60½" wide. Trim 2 of the 3½" x 70" cream strips to this measurement. Sew them to the top and bottom of the quilt; press the seams toward the borders.

2 Measure the length of your quilt, including the borders you just added. It should measure approximately 66½" long. Trim the remaining 3½" x 70" cream strips to this measurement and sew them to the sides of the quilt top; press the seams toward the borders.

Sawtooth Border

1 Mark a diagonal line from corner to corner on the wrong side of the 3⅞" cream squares.

2 Place each of the cream squares right sides together with a 3⅞" burgundy square. Stitch ¼" away from each side of the drawn line. Cut along the marked line and press the seam toward the burgundy triangles to complete 88 triangle squares measuring 3½" x 3½".

Make 88.

3 Each of the 4 borders is made with 22 triangle squares. In each border, the triangles change direction in the middle of the border. For each border, join 11 triangle squares together with the burgundy triangles facing to the left and another set of 11 units with the burgundy triangles facing to the right. Then join the 2 sets together to create a large cream triangle in the middle of the border.

Make 4 borders.

4 Stitch a pieced border to the top and bottom of the quilt top, with the base of the burgundy triangles toward the center of the quilt. Press the seams toward the inner cream border.

5 Sew a 3½" cream square to each end of the 2 remaining pieced borders and press the seams toward the squares. Stitch the borders to the opposite sides of the quilt top with the base of the burgundy triangles toward the center of the quilt. Press.

Outer Border

1 Measure the width of the quilt as in step 1 of "Inner Border," opposite. Trim 2 of the 6½" x 90" cream strips to this length (approximately 72½") and sew them to the top and bottom of the quilt. Press the seams toward the outer borders.

2 Measure the length of the quilt as in step 2 of "Inner Border." Trim the 2 remaining border strips to that length (approximately 84½") and sew them to the opposite sides of the quilt top. Press the seams toward the outer borders.

Finishing

1 Cut the backing fabric into 3 equal lengths, remove the selvages, and join the 3 pieces together side by side to make a backing with vertical seams. Press the seams to one side.

2 Layer the backing, batting, and quilt top, smoothing each layer from the center outward as you go. Baste the layers together at 4" intervals.

3 Hand or machine quilt as desired. Diane's quilt was professionally machine quilted by Michelle Breeze of Licorice Lane using an allover tulip-shaped quilting pattern.

4 Remove the basting and trim the edges of the quilt, leaving ¼" of batting and backing beyond the pieced quilt top to fill the binding. Join the 2¼"-wide binding strips end to end; press the seams open. Attach the binding to the quilt, referring to "Binding" on page 94 for more details.

5 Label your quilt, including your name, the date, and any other relevant information.

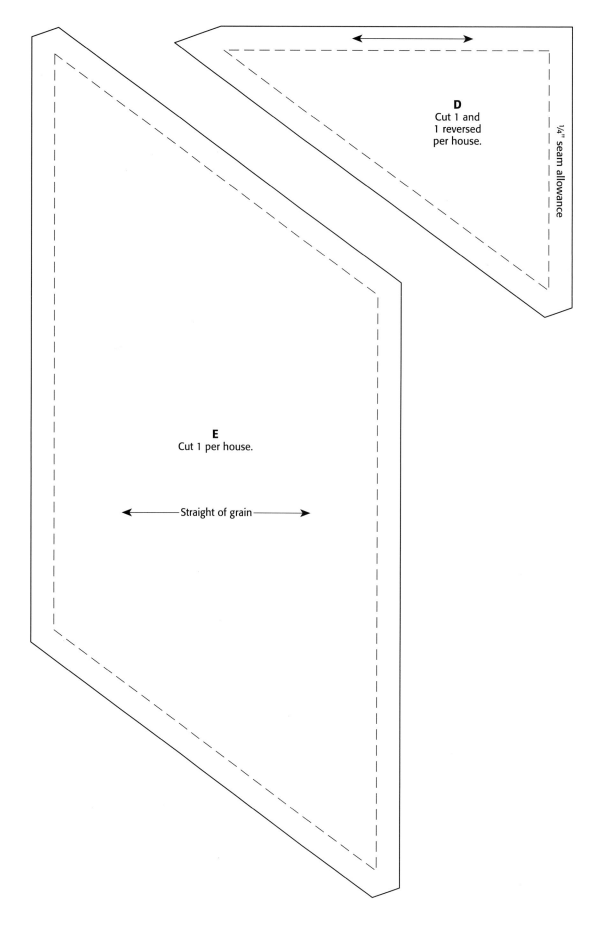

D
Cut 1 and
1 reversed
per house.

¼" seam allowance

E
Cut 1 per house.

←——Straight of grain——→

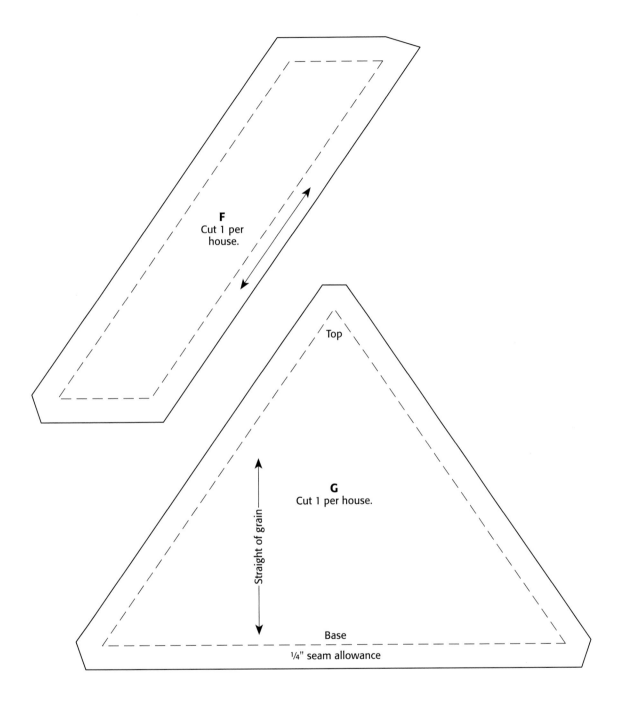

F
Cut 1 per
house.

G
Cut 1 per house.

Top

Straight of grain

Base

¼" seam allowance

STARS IN MY GARDEN

This quilt by Tracey Browning is ideal for a friendship-block swap or as a way to use up charm squares. The Hunter's Star block incorporates foundation piecing for accurate piecing of otherwise tricky shapes. The floral vine border is easy to do with fusible appliqué.

Tracey arranged the blocks with the colors gradated from lighter and warmer ones in the top left corner to darker and cooler ones in the bottom right corner of the quilt. You can follow this plan or move your blocks around in a random arrangement.

MATERIALS
Yardages are based on 42"-wide (107 cm) fabric.

◆ ⅝ yd. (60 cm) of black solid for outer border and binding

◆ ⅜ yd. of white-on-white print for block background

◆ ¼ yd. (20 cm) of purple for inner border

◆ Fat quarter *each* of 2 green prints for appliqués

◆ Scraps of 24 assorted jewel-tone fabrics (at least 4" or 10 cm square) for blocks and appliqués

◆ ¾ yd. (70 cm) of backing fabric

◆ 23" x 29" (60 cm x 75 cm) piece of batting

◆ Fine-point permanent marker

◆ ½ yd. (40 cm) of lightweight interfacing or paper for foundations

◆ ¼ yd. (20 cm) of fusible web

◆ Embroidery floss to match appliqué fabrics

Machine pieced and hand quilted by Tracey Browning.

Finished Block Size: 3" x 3" (7.5 cm square)
Finished Quilt Size: 21½" x 27½" (55 cm x 70 cm)

CUTTING

All cutting dimensions include ¼" seam allowances. Instructions are for cutting strips across the fabric width except where noted. The Hunter's Star foundation pattern and the patterns for the appliqué flower and leaf are on page 53.

From the 24 jewel-tone scraps, cut:
◆ 24 squares, 4" x 4"

From the white-on-white print, cut:
◆ 3 strips, 4" x 42"; crosscut into 24 squares, 4" x 4"

From the purple fabric, cut:
◆ 2 strips, 2" x 42". From each strip cut one 2" x 18½" strip and one 2" x 15½" strip.

From the black fabric, cut:
◆ 4 strips, 3½" x 21½"

◆ 3 strips, 2" x 42"

BLOCK ASSEMBLY

1 Place a jewel-tone square right sides together with a background square. Referring to the diagram, measure and mark 2½" in both directions from the corner of the squares and cut diagonally across the corner to produce the jewel-tone and white triangles for position 1 of the foundation.

Measure over 1¼" and make another cut to create strips for positions 2 and 3. The remaining triangle is for position 4. Repeat with the remaining 23 sets of squares. Each set of 4" squares will yield one 3" Hunter's Star block.

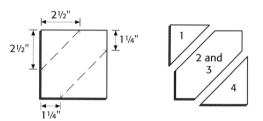

2 Using the permanent marker, trace 48 half blocks from the foundation pattern onto the interfacing or foundation paper. Note that the cutting line is the outer dotted line and the inner solid lines are the sewing lines. The numbers indicate order of piecing. Mark all lines and numbers onto each foundation. For foundation piecing, place the fabrics underneath the unmarked side of the foundation and sew on the side with the lines drawn on it.

3 Place a small white triangle right side up over position 1 on the underside of the foundation. Hold it up to the light if necessary to ensure that the fabric extends beyond the seam allowance and pin it in place. Place the strip of jewel-tone fabric right side down on top of the triangle and flip the entire unit over while holding the fabrics and foundation with your thumb and forefinger.

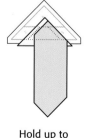

Hold up to
light and align.

50

4 Stitch along the line between positions 1 and 2, beginning and ending the stitching slightly beyond each end of the line. Remove the foundation from your machine and open out the jewel-tone strip to make sure that it covers position 2 on the foundation.

Stitch, paper side up.

5 Fold the fabrics and foundation out of the way so you can trim the seam allowance to a scant ¼". Then open out the strip and iron or finger-press the seam, taking care that the fabric is not creased or pleated along the seam. Trim the strip so that it extends at least ¼" beyond the lines for position 2.

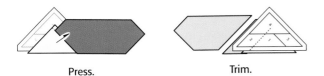

Press.   Trim.

6 Add the remainder of the jewel-tone strip to position 3 in the same manner, referring to the diagram below. The large white triangle is added last to complete the half block.

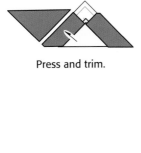

Press and trim.

Align and stitch
trimmed scrap.

Add piece 4.   Press.

7 Piece the other half of the block in the same manner, beginning with the small triangle of jewel-tone fabric and placing the white and jewel-tone fabric in the opposite positions to the first half block.

8 Press both the half blocks, and then turn them over for trimming. Using a rotary-cutting ruler, line up the ¼" mark with the outer seamline on the foundation block and trim away the excess fabric. Trim on each side of the half blocks.

9 Join the 2 half-block triangles. Press the block and then, using your ruler and rotary cutter, trim the dog-ears to create a 3½" block.

10 Repeat steps 3–8 to make the remaining 23 blocks.

QUILT ASSEMBLY

1 Lay out the Hunter's Star blocks in 6 rows of 4 blocks each, referring to the quilt photograph, opposite, to ensure the correct rotation of each block. In the quilt shown, the blocks are arranged with the colors gradated from the lightest fabrics in the upper left corner to the darkest fabrics in the bottom right corner of the quilt.

2 Sew the blocks together in rows. Join the rows together, carefully matching the block intersections and seams.

BORDERS

The quilt has an inner purple border and a wider outer black border that is appliquéd.

Inner Border

1 Measure the length of your quilt; it should measure approximately 18½" long. Sew the 2" x 18½" purple strips to the sides of the quilt top, easing if necessary to fit.

2 Measure the width of your quilt, including the side borders you've just added; it should measure approximately 15½" wide. Join the 2" x 15½" purple strips to the top and bottom of the quilt top, easing to fit if necessary.

Outer Border

1 Join the 3½" x 21½" black borders to the quilt top in the same manner as you did the first border strips, adding the side borders first and then the top and bottom borders.

2 Using the two different green prints, cut 1"-wide bias strips totaling 110" in length.

3 Sew the strips together with diagonal seams to form a continuous strip. Then, fold the strip in half lengthwise with wrong sides together and stitch a ⅛" seam along the length to form a tube. Press the vine so the seam is off-center at the back of the tube, ensuring the raw edges do not protrude at the sides.

4 Referring to the quilt photograph, place the bias vine on the border. Note that Tracey followed the colorwash effect of her quilt blocks and placed the dark part of the vine on the right and bottom borders and the light part of the vine on the left and top borders.

Pin-mark each side of the quilt top into quarters and curve the vine gently using these points as a guide. Make sure to keep the vine within the seam allowance at the outside edges of the quilt. Once you are happy with the placement, pin and then appliqué the vine in place by hand or machine using matching thread.

5 Trace 28 flowers, 28 flower centers, and 48 leaves using the patterns on page 53 onto the paper side of fusible web. Cut out the shapes about ¼" beyond the drawn lines.

TIP — It is easier to draw all your flower centers close together and then fuse them to the selected fabric as a whole group. You can do the same with the leaves to save cutting time and a bit of fabric.

6 Press the fusible-web shapes to the wrong side of your selected fabrics and cut them out on the drawn lines.

7 Peel the paper backing off the appliqués and arrange them on the black border. When you are satisfied with the arrangement, press to fuse them in place.

8 Blanket stitch around each appliqué by hand or machine. For hand sewing, use 1 strand of embroidery floss.

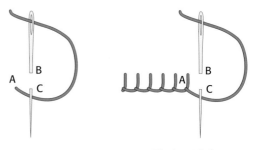

Blanket Stitch

FINISHING

1 Trim the backing fabric and batting so they are about 4" larger than the quilt top in each direction.

2 Layer the backing, batting, and quilt top, smoothing each layer from the center outward as you go. Baste the layers together at 4" intervals.

3 Hand or machine quilt as desired. Tracey outline quilted each star by hand, quilting ¼" around the outside of the stars using ¼" masking tape as a guide. She quilted a diamond pattern in the purple border, again using masking tape to mark the pattern, and quilting on either side of the tape. In the black border, Tracey used 2 shades of green thread to coordinate with the vine and leaf fabrics and outline quilted around those motifs.

4 Remove the basting and trim the edges of the quilt, leaving ¼" of batting and backing beyond the pieced quilt top to fill the binding. Join the 2"-wide black binding strips end to end; press the seams open. Attach the binding to the quilt, referring to "Binding" on page 94 for more details.

5 Label your quilt, including your name, the date, and any other relevant information.

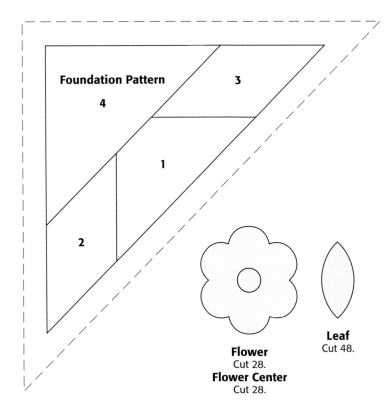

Foundation Pattern

4

3

1

2

Flower
Cut 28.
Flower Center
Cut 28.

Leaf
Cut 48.

ROAD TO THE MOUNTAINS

Inspired by an antique quilt, Ruth Buchanan used some favorite fabrics from her stash for this stunning, simple-to-make scrap quilt. Choose rich, muted colors to create this classic quilt for display on a wall or on a bed.

The block featured is known by several names, most commonly as Jacob's Ladder. This setting uses it in "positive" and "negative" forms for graphic impact. Rotary cutting and machine piecing make this project quite simple for beginners.

MATERIALS
Yardages are based on 42"-wide (107 cm) fabric.

- 36 fat eighths of assorted medium and dark prints for blocks
- 3⅝ yds. (3.4 m) of muslin for blocks and border
- ⅔ yd. (60 cm) of red print for binding
- 4¾ yds. (4.5 m) of backing fabric
- 83" x 83" (211 cm square) piece of batting

*Machine pieced by Ruth Buchanan.
Machine quilted by Wil Heinrichs of Quiltstuff
Hand-Guided Machine Quilting Service.*

Finished Block Size: 12" x 12" (30.5 cm square)
Finished Quilt Size: 76½" x 76½" (195 cm square)

CUTTING

All cutting dimensions include ¼" seam allowances.
Instructions are for cutting strips across the fabric
width except where noted.

From the muslin, cut:

◆ 23 strips, 2½" x 42"; crosscut into 360 squares,
2½" x 2½"

◆ 9 strips, 4⅞" x 42"; crosscut into 72 squares,
4⅞" x 4⅞". Cut each square once diagonally to
yield 144 triangles.

◆ 8 border strips, 2½" x 42"

From *each* of the 36 medium and dark prints, cut:

◆ 2 squares, 4⅞" x 4⅞"; cut each square once
diagonally to yield 4 triangles (144 total)

◆ 10 squares, 2½" x 2½" (360 total)

From the red print cut:

◆ 8 strips, 2½" x 42"

BLOCK ASSEMBLY

This quilt contains 36 blocks: 18 positive blocks,
with the print squares across the center of the block,
and 18 negative blocks, with muslin squares across
the center of the block. Divide your printed fabrics
into two piles, so there are roughly even numbers of
each color in each pile. This will serve to scatter the
colors among the positive and negative blocks.

Each block requires 10 muslin squares, 10 print
squares, 4 muslin triangles, and 4 print triangles.

1 Stitch the muslin and print squares into pairs and
then sew the pairs together to make four-patch
units.

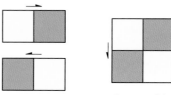

Make 5 per block.

2 Sew the muslin and print triangles together and
press the seams toward the print fabric.

Make 4 per block.

3 Sew the units together to create rows and then stitch the rows together to complete a block. Repeat, making a total of 18 positive and 18 negative blocks. Each type of block uses the same number of pieces; only the arrangement of the colors is changed.

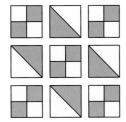

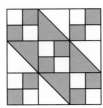

Positive Block
Make 18.

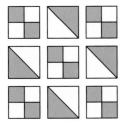

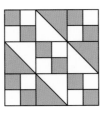

Negative Block
Make 18.

TIP — While this quilt has been made in warm country colors, it would also look wonderful made with rich hand-dyed fabrics against a black background.

QUILT ASSEMBLY

1 Referring to the quilt photograph, opposite, as a guide, lay out the blocks in 6 rows of 6 blocks each on your design wall or floor. Take care to position the blocks so all the positive blocks run in one direction and the negative blocks are at right angles to them, running in the opposite diagonal.

TIP — Ruth suggests checking the layout through a door peephole or reducing glass to make sure that the colors and prints are scattered and that the effect is pleasing.

2 Sew the blocks together into horizontal rows, matching the seam intersections. Press the seams in alternate rows in opposite directions.

3 Stitch the rows together, matching all seam intersections, and then gently press the quilt top.

BORDER

1 Sew the eight 2½" x 42" muslin border strips together into 4 pairs.

2 Measure the length of your quilt; it should be approximately 72½" long. Trim 2 of the long border strips to this length and join them to the sides of your quilt top. Press the seams toward the borders.

3 Measure the width of the quilt; it should be approximately 76½" wide. Trim the remaining 2 long border strips to this length and join them to the top and bottom of the quilt top. Press the seams toward the borders.

FINISHING

1 Cut the backing fabric into 2 equal lengths, remove the selvages, and join the 2 pieces together side by side to make a backing with vertical seams. Press the seams to one side.

2 Layer the backing, batting, and quilt top, smoothing each layer from the center outward as you go. Baste the layers together at 4" intervals.

3 Hand or machine quilt as desired. Ruth's quilt was professionally machine quilted with a non-directional, continuous-line pattern in a muted mustard-colored thread.

4 Remove the basting and trim the edges of the quilt, leaving ¼" of batting and backing beyond the pieced quilt top to fill the binding. Join the 2½"-wide binding strips end to end; press the seams open. Attach the binding to the quilt, referring to "Binding" on page 94 for more details.

5 Label your quilt, including your name, the date, and any other relevant information.

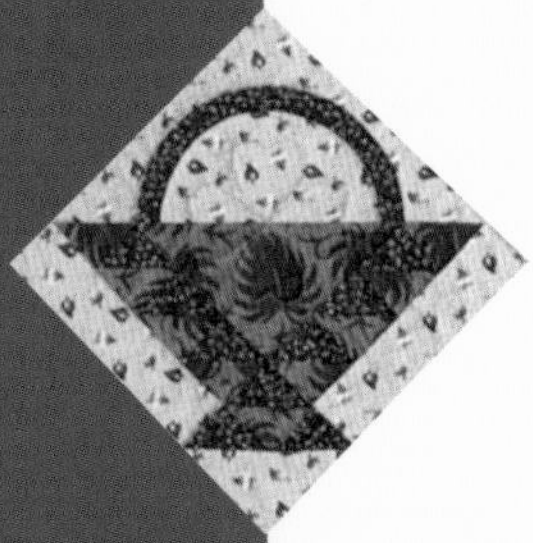

AUTUMN BASKETS

Cindy Cudmore chose a combination of high contrast and blended fabric colors for this fall-inspired quilt. Two different basket styles are showcased nicely between vertical sashing strips. What could be more appropriate for autumn than rows of lovely baskets, which conjure up thoughts of gathering bountiful harvests?

MATERIALS

Yardages are based on 42"-wide (107 cm) fabric.

◆ 2¼ yds. (2 m) of plum print for inner and outer borders, binding, and baskets

◆ 2 yds. (1.8 m) of large-scale rose print for middle border and baskets

◆ 1⅔ yds. (1.5 m) of green print for narrow sashing

◆ 1⅔ yds. (1.5 m) of dark tan print for wide sashing and baskets

◆ ⅓ yd. (30 cm) *each* of 8 assorted light prints for block backgrounds

◆ 1 yd. (90 cm) of light tan for setting triangles

◆ ¼ yd. (20 cm) *each* of 12 assorted dark prints for baskets

◆ Fat eighth *each* of 6 assorted medium prints for baskets

◆ 4⅜ yds. (4 m) of backing fabric

◆ 66" x 76" (170 cm x 193 cm) piece of batting

◆ Fine-point permanent marker

◆ Template plastic

◆ Fusible web (optional)

Pieced and machine quilted by Cindy Cudmore.

Finished Block Size: 7½" x 7½" (19 cm square)
Finished Quilt Size: 57½" x 68⅛" (146 cm x 173 cm)

CUTTING

All cutting dimensions include ¼" seam allowances. Instructions are for cutting strips across the fabric width except for the borders and sashing, which are cut on the lengthwise grain. Cut these pieces first; then use the leftovers—along with the assorted dark and medium prints—for the basket blocks.

From the light tan print, cut:
- 2 strips, 11⅞" x 42"; crosscut into 6 squares, 11⅞" x 11⅞". Cut each square on both diagonals to yield 24 triangles.
- 1 strip, 6¼" x 42; crosscut into 6 squares, 6¼" x 6¼". Cut each square once diagonally to yield 12 triangles.

From the green print, cut:
- 6 strips, 1½" x 53¾"
- 2 strips, 1½" x 45¼"

From the dark tan print, cut:
- 2 strips, 3¾" x 53¾"
- 1 square, 5⅞" x 5⅞"; cut in half once diagonally

From the plum print, cut:
- 2 strips, 1¼" x 54¼"
- 2 strips, 1¼" x 46½"
- 2 strips, 1½" x 66¾"
- 2 strips, 1½" x 57½"
- 4 strips, 2½" x 72"

From the large-scale rose print, cut:
- 2 strips, 5" x 57¾"
- 2 strips, 5" x 55½"

Block 1

For each block 1 (appliquéd handle), choose 2 contrasting medium or dark prints and 1 light background print. Remember to include the leftover border fabrics with your other medium and dark prints.

Note: The cutting for the basket blocks is given for one block at a time. You will have leftover pieces from each block, so you may mix and match them with other blocks as desired for a scrappier look.

From 1 medium or dark print, cut:
- 1 square, 4⅝" x 4⅝"; cut in half once diagonally to yield 2 triangles (you'll have 1 extra)
- 5 squares, 2⅛" x 2⅛"; cut in half once diagonally to yield 10 triangles (you'll have 1 extra)

From the other medium or dark print, cut:
- 5 squares, 2⅛" x 2⅛"; cut in half once diagonally to yield 10 triangles (you'll have 1 extra)
- 1 basket handle, using the pattern on page 63

From the light print, cut:
- 2 rectangles, 1¾" x 5½"
- 1 square, 3⅜" x 3⅜"; cut in half once diagonally to yield 2 triangles (you'll have 1 extra)
- 1 square, 7⅛" x 7⅛"; cut in half once diagonally to yield 2 triangles (you'll have 1 extra)

Block 2

For each block 2 (pieced handle), choose 2 contrasting medium or dark prints and 1 light background print.

From 1 medium or dark print, cut:
- 6 squares, 2⅛" x 2⅛"; cut in half once diagonally to yield 12 triangles (you'll have 1 extra)

From the other medium or dark print, cut:

◆ 1 square, 5⅞" x 5⅞"; cut in half once diagonally to yield 2 triangles (you'll have 1 extra)

From the light print, cut:

◆ 5 squares, 2⅛" x 2⅛"; cut in half once diagonally to yield 10 triangles (you'll have 1 extra)

◆ 1 square, 5⅞" x 5⅞"; cut in half once diagonally to yield 2 triangles (you'll have 1 extra)

◆ 2 rectangles, 1¾" x 5½"

◆ 1 square, 3⅜" x 3⅜"; cut in half once diagonally to yield 2 triangles (you'll have 1 extra)

BLOCK 1 ASSEMBLY

Gather the pieces for one block at a time to avoid confusion. Keep the other pieces in individual plastic bags or envelopes until you're ready for them.

1 Trace the handle pattern onto template plastic and cut it out carefully on the line. The basket handle has a ¼" seam allowance added to the bottom edges so they will be caught in the seam when the basket block is assembled.
If you plan to hand appliqué your basket handles, trace around the template onto one of your contrasting medium or dark prints selected for the block and cut out about ⅛" away from the curved lines for a seam allowance. If you'll be fusing your handles, trace around the template onto fusible web and then prepare your basket handles referring to "Fusible Appliqué" on page 92.

2 Stitch the 2⅛" contrasting triangles together in pairs to make 7 triangle squares. Press the seams toward the lighter fabric. Stitch 4 triangle squares together for the left side of the basket and 3 triangle squares together for the right side, as shown. Then add the remaining 2⅛" triangles to the end of each strip and press the seams toward the triangles.

Left Side

Right Side

3 Join the 3-square strip to the right side of the 4⅝" triangle. Press the seam toward the large triangle, and then join the 4-square strip to the left side of the large triangle; press as before.

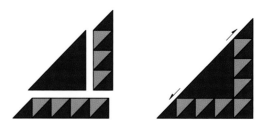

4 Stitch a 2⅛" triangle of the dark or medium fabric to one end of each of the 1¾" x 5½" light rectangles. Press the seams toward the rectangles. Stitch these to the adjacent sides of the pieced basket section and press the seams toward the rectangles.

Make 1.   Make 1.

5 Sew the 3⅜" light triangle to the bottom of the basket and press the seam toward the triangle.

6 Position the handle from step 1 in the 7⅛" light triangle and appliqué it in place using your favorite method. If you're stitching by hand or machine, stitch the outer curve first and then the inner curve, clipping the seam as required.

7 Pin the top edge of the pieced basket to the appliquéd triangle; then stitch and press the seam toward the light triangle.

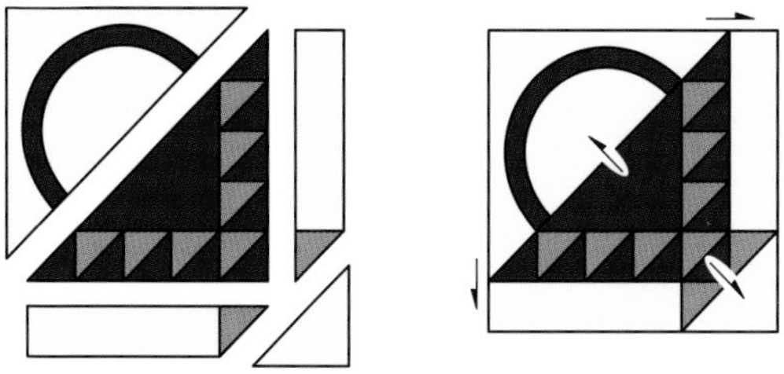

8 Repeat steps 2–7 to make a total of 8 blocks with appliquéd handles.

BLOCK 2 ASSEMBLY

Gather the pieces for one block at a time to avoid confusion. Keep the other pieces in individual plastic bags or envelopes until you're ready for them.

1 Stitch the 2⅛" light and the 2⅛" medium or dark triangles together into 9 triangle squares. Press the seams toward the light fabric. Stitch 4 triangle squares together into 1 unit for the right handle and 5 triangle squares together for the left handle, taking care to orient the triangles as shown.

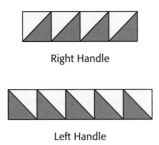

Right Handle

Left Handle

2 Stitch the 5⅞" light and the 5⅞" medium or dark triangles together and press the seam toward the darker fabric. Sew the shorter pieced strip from step 1 to one side of the light triangle and press the seam toward the light triangle. Then join the longer pieced strip to the opposite side of the light triangle. Press.

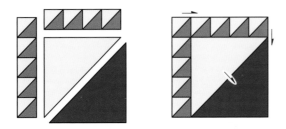

3 Sew a 2⅛" medium or dark triangle to each of the light rectangles and then join the rectangles to the block. To complete the basket, sew the 3⅜" light triangle across the bottom of the basket and press the seam toward the triangle.

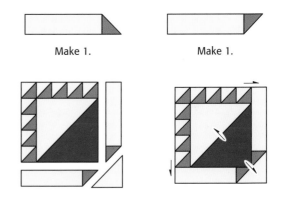

Make 1.   Make 1.

4 Repeat steps 1–3 to make a total of 7 blocks with pieced handles.

QUILT ASSEMBLY

1 Lay out the basket blocks in a vertical row, beginning with a pieced-handle basket and alternating with appliquéd-handle baskets, as shown. Position the light tan 11⅞" setting triangles and the 6¼" corner triangles as shown. Sew the triangles to the blocks and press the seams toward the triangles. Then sew the diagonal rows together, carefully matching the seam intersections as you go.

2 Make 2 more vertical rows, this time starting with an appliquéd-handle basket and alternating appliquéd- and pieced-handle blocks. Attach the setting triangles in the same manner as for the first row.

3 Stitch a 1½" x 53¾" green sashing strip to both sides of each vertical block row and press the seams toward the strips.

Center Row

4 Join the 3 vertical rows of blocks together with the 3¾" x 53¾" dark tan sashing strips between the block rows.

5 Stitch the 1½" x 45¼" green sashing strips to the top and bottom of the quilt top and press the seams toward the green strips.

BORDERS

1 Measure the length of your quilt and trim the 1¼" x 54¼" plum border strips to fit if necessary. Sew the strips to opposite sides of the quilt top. Press the seams toward the borders.

2 Measure the width of your quilt and trim the 1¼" x 46½" plum border strips to fit if necessary. Sew the strips to the top and bottom of the quilt top and press the seams toward the borders.

3 For the middle large-scale rose border, measure the quilt top as before and trim the border strips to fit if necessary. Stitch the 5" x 57¾" strips to the sides and then sew the 5" x 55½" strips to the top and bottom of the quilt top in the same manner as for the inner plum border.

4 For the outer border, stitch the 1½" x 66¾" plum strips to the sides of the quilt top and the 1½" x 57½" strips to the top and bottom edges, measuring the borders to fit in the same manner as for the other borders. Press the seams toward the outer borders.

FINISHING

1 Cut the backing fabric into 2 equal lengths, remove the selvages, and join the 2 pieces together side by side to make a backing with a vertical seam. Press the seam to one side.

2 Layer the backing, batting, and quilt top, smoothing each layer from the center outward as you go. Baste the layers together at 4" intervals.

3 Hand or machine quilt as desired. Cindy machine quilted her quilt in the ditch along both sides of each green sashing strip, as well as in the ditch around each basket and handle and outer block edge. Four hearts are quilted in the center of each basket. Cindy quilted a clamshell pattern on the setting and corner triangles and a cable through the middle of the dark tan sashing strips. The middle and outer borders are quilted with a Baptist fan design.

4 Remove the basting and trim the edges of the quilt, leaving ¼" of batting and backing beyond the pieced quilt top to fill the binding. Join the 2½"-wide plum binding strips end to end; press the seams open. Attach the binding to the quilt, referring to "Binding" on page 94 for more details.

5 Label your quilt, including your name, the date, and any other relevant information.

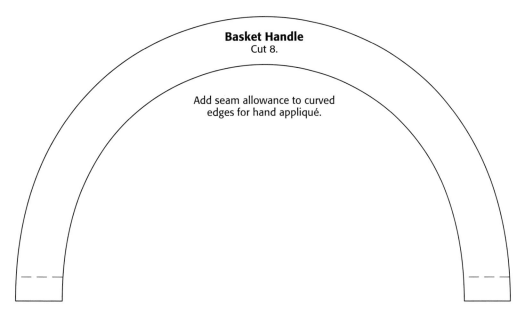

Basket Handle
Cut 8.

Add seam allowance to curved edges for hand appliqué.

MANDALA

This glorious design shows the flexibility of the ever-popular Drunkard's Path block, which happens to be one of Jacky Hens's favorites. She used a variety of light- and dark-value floral prints to create an interesting diamond pattern, and you'll find it provides a great way to use all of those small scraps in your collection.

While Jacky used floral fabrics for her quilt, this pattern would look equally stunning made using just two contrasting fabrics.

MATERIALS

Yardages are based on 42"-wide (107 cm) fabric.

- 6⅜ yds. (5.8 m) of assorted light scraps for blocks
- 5⅞ yds. (5.4 m) of assorted floral scraps for blocks and binding
- 8⅜ yds. (7.6 m) of backing fabric
- 99" x 99" (251 cm square) piece of batting
- Template plastic
- Fine-point permanent marker
- Lead pencil

Machine pieced and quilted by Jacky Hens.

Finished Block Size: 22½" x 22½" (57.2 cm square)
Finished Quilt Size: 91" x 91" (231 cm square)

CUTTING

All cutting dimensions include ¼" seam allowances. Instructions are for cutting strips across the fabric width except where noted.

From the floral scraps, cut:

◆ 320 of piece A

◆ 256 of piece B

◆ 3"-wide strips to total 380" in length

From the light scraps, cut:

◆ 256 of piece A

◆ 320 of piece B

TIP — Make templates for the A and B pieces using the patterns, opposite. Transfer all markings onto your templates, including the grain lines. Keep the straight edges of the templates on the grain line of the fabric and trace around them with a pencil onto the wrong side of your selected fabrics.

Be sure also to transfer the pinning reference marks onto the curved edges of your fabric pieces before cutting out the A and B pieces. Matching these marks when sewing is important and will help you achieve smooth, pucker-free curves.

BLOCK ASSEMBLY

You will need to make a total of 576 units—320 with a floral piece A and a light piece B and 256 with a light piece A and a floral piece B. The units are then assembled into 12 blocks and 8 half blocks.

1 Stitch pairs of A and B pieces together, each time pairing a floral with a light piece. With the A piece on top and with right sides together, pin the center of the curves; then pin the sides and quarters, making sure to keep the side edges together as shown. Ease the B fabric around the curve. When finished stitching, press the seam toward the darker fabric.

Make 320.   Make 256.

2 Using a design wall or the floor, arrange the units in blocks and half blocks. Each full block consists of 36 pieced units—16 with floral B pieces and 20 with light B pieces. Each half block consists of 18 units—8 with floral B pieces and 10 with light B pieces.

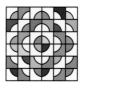

Full Block   Half Block

3 When you are pleased with the fabric and color distribution within a block, stitch the units together. To make assembly easier, join the units into nine-patch units first. Each nine-patch unit is a quarter block. Press the seams as shown to reduce bulk, and then stitch the nine-patch units together to complete full and half blocks.

Make a total of 12 blocks and 8 half blocks.

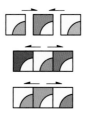

Quarter Block

QUILT ASSEMBLY

1 Referring to the quilt layout, position the blocks in 4 rows. Each row begins and ends with a half block and contains 3 full blocks.

2 Sew the blocks and half blocks together in rows, and then join the rows. Press the quilt top.

FINISHING

1 Cut the backing fabric into 3 equal lengths, remove the selvages, and join the 3 pieces together side by side to make a backing with vertical seams. Press the seams to one side.

2 Layer the backing, batting, and quilt top, smoothing each layer from the center outward as you go. Baste the layers together at 4" intervals.

3 Hand or machine quilt as desired. Jacky machine quilted in the ditch around the Drunkard's Path units and hand quilted circles in the light areas where the corners of the blocks are joined.

4 Remove the basting and trim the edges of the quilt, leaving ¼" of batting and backing beyond the pieced quilt top to fill the binding. Join the varying lengths of the 3"-wide floral binding strips end to end using diagonal seams; press the seams open. You will need to make a strip about 380" long. Press the seams open and press the binding in half lengthwise wrong sides together. Attach the binding to the quilt, referring to "Binding" on page 94 for more details.

5 Label your quilt, including your name, the date, and any other relevant information.

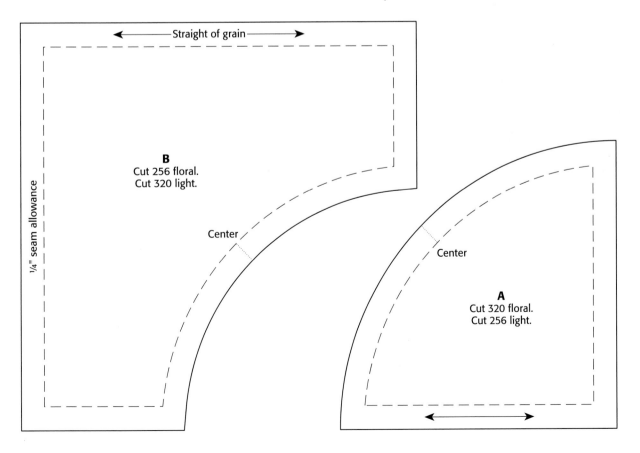

PRAIRIE MEADOW

Becky Peters replicated an original quilt design by Adrienne Franklin to display the beautiful Prairie Meadow collection of fabric from Quilting Treasures by Cranston. You, too, can make your own rendition of the project by selecting your favorite floral prints. A subtle blend of background fabrics, easy large-scale piecing, and focal-point appliqué all combine in a romantic and inviting quilt.

MATERIALS

Yardages are based on 42"-wide (107 cm) fabric.

- 2⅔ yds. (2.4 m) of large-scale floral green print for patchwork and borders
- 2¼ yds. (2 m) of lavender print for appliqué, patchwork, borders, and binding
- 2¼ yds. (2 m) of pink print for appliqué, patchwork, and borders
- 1 yd. (90 cm) of green print for leaves and stems
- ⅞ yd. (80 cm) *each* of 4 assorted ecru tone-on-tone prints for appliqué background and patchwork
- ⅞ yd. (80 cm) of light blue print for appliqué and patchwork
- ⅝ yd. (60 cm) of small-scale floral green print for patchwork
- 5 yds. (4.6 m) of backing fabric
- 72" x 89" (183 cm x 226 cm) piece of batting
- Template plastic
- Fine-point permanent marker

Designed by Adrienne Franklin, pieced and appliquéd by Becky Peters, machine quilted by Michelle Breeze of Licorice Lane Designs.

Finished Block Sizes:
   Appliqué Tulips: 12" x 12" (30.5 cm square)
   Pinwheels: 8" x 8" (20 cm square)
Finished Quilt Size: 68" x 85" (173 cm x 216 cm)

Cutting

All cutting dimensions include ¼" seam allowances. Instructions are for cutting strips across the fabric width except where noted.

From the light blue print, cut:
- 3 strips, 5⅛" x 42"; crosscut into 16 squares, 5⅛" x 5⅛"
- 1 strip, 4¾" x 42"; crosscut into 8 squares, 4¾" x 4¾"
- 1 strip, 5" x 42"; crosscut into 8 squares, 5" x 5". From the squares, cut:
   - 7 of piece A
   - 1 of piece B

From the lavender print, cut on the lengthwise grain:
- 2 strips, 2½" x 72"
- 2 strips, 2½" x 54"

From the width of the remaining lavender print, cut:
- 2 strips, 4¾" x 42"; crosscut into 12 squares, 4¾" x 4¾"
- 2 strips, 5⅛" x 42"; crosscut into 8 squares, 5⅛" x 5⅛"
- 2 strips, 5" x 42"; crosscut into 9 squares, 5" x 5". From the squares, cut:
   - 2 of piece A
   - 6 of piece B
- 10 strips, 3" x 42"

From the pink print, cut on the lengthwise grain:
- 2 strips, 1½" x 72"
- 2 strips, 1½" x 54"

From the remaining pink print, cut on the crosswise grain:
- 1 strip, 4¾" x 42"; crosscut into 4 squares, 4¾" x 4¾"
- 2 strips, 5" x 42"; crosscut into 8 squares, 5" x 5". From the squares, cut:
   - 7 of piece A
   - 1 of piece B

From the green print, cut:
- 58 of piece D
- 1 strip, 12" x 42"; from this strip cut 18 bias strips, 1¼" wide

From the width of *each* of the 4 ecru prints, cut:
- 1 strip, 5⅛" x 42"; crosscut into 8 squares, 5⅛" x 5⅛" (32 squares total)
- 2 strips, 8½" x 42"; crosscut into 6 squares, 8½" x 8½" (24 squares total)

From one of the ecru prints, cut:
- 1 square, 18¼" x 18¼"; cut the square diagonally in both directions for the appliqué triangles. (Only 2 triangles are needed; you'll have 2 extra.)

70

From the large-scale floral green print, cut:

◆ 1 strip, 18¼" x 42"; crosscut 2 squares, 18¼" x 18¼". Cut each square on both diagonals to yield 8 triangles (F).

From the *length* of the remaining large-scale floral green print, cut:

◆ 2 strips, 6" x 72"

◆ 2 strips, 6" x 54"

◆ 1 strip, 9⅜" x length of fabric; crosscut into 6 squares, 9⅜" x 9⅜". Cut each square once diagonally to yield 12 triangles (E).

From the small-scale floral green print, cut:

◆ 2 strips, 5⅛" x 42"; crosscut into 8 squares, 5⅛" x 5⅛". Cut each square once diagonally to yield 16 triangles (G).

◆ 2 strips, 5⅛" x 42"; crosscut into 8 squares, 5⅛" x 5⅛"

◆ 1 of piece C

APPLIQUÉ BLOCK ASSEMBLY

1 Trace appliqué patterns A, B, C, and D on pages 72–73 onto template plastic. Label each template and cut them out on the drawn lines. Mark an X at the base of each leaf. All templates are finished size; add a seam allowance when cutting out fabric for hand appliqué. No seam allowances are needed for fusible web. Refer to "Cutting," opposite, for the number to cut of each shape.

2 Join the 8½" ecru squares into 6 Four Patch blocks, using one of each of the fabrics per block. Lay out the blocks on point, referring to the quilt photo. Rotate them for a pleasing balance of tones and place a pin at the bottom corner of each so that you'll orient your appliqué in the right direction. The blocks will be trimmed to 12½" square after completing the appliqué.

3 Fold each 1¼" bias strip wrong sides together and finger-press the fold. Open out the strip and then fold each raw edge to meet at the center fold. Fold the strip again to make a stem with folded

edges on both sides. Referring to the block diagram, pin the stems to the background blocks and baste them with a running stitch. Stitch the stems in place, turning an angled edge under at the bottom of each one. The flowers will cover the raw edges at the top.

4 Appliqué the leaves and then each of the A and B flowers, using threads to match the appliqué fabrics. Make sure all appliqués are within the 12" x 12" area of your finished block size. Repeat to complete 6 Tulip blocks. Trim each completed block to 12½" square.

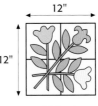

Make 6.

5 Use the ecru triangles cut from the 18¼" square to make 2 appliqué triangles. Position and stitch the flowers and leaves, ensuring that the pieces do not encroach into the seam allowance areas.

Make 2.

PINWHEEL BLOCK ASSEMBLY

1 Mark a diagonal line from corner to corner on the wrong side of each 5⅛" ecru square. Place the squares right sides together with the 5⅛" colored squares. You should have 8 pairs with lavender squares, 8 pairs with small-scale green floral print squares, and 16 pairs with light blue squares. Sew ¼" away from either side of the diagonal line and then cut the squares apart on the centerline. Press the seams toward the darker fabrics.

2 Join the triangle squares to make 8 light blue,
4 lavender, and 4 green Pinwheel blocks, as
shown.

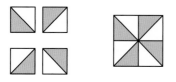

QUILT ASSEMBLY

1 Join 4 of the Tulip blocks together with the stems
all pointing to the center as shown in the quilt
photograph. Appliqué piece C over the center
intersection of the blocks. This center section
should measure 24½" square.

2 To make the large pieced setting triangles, sew
the pink, light blue, and lavender squares together
with the G setting triangles, as shown. Make 4
triangle units.

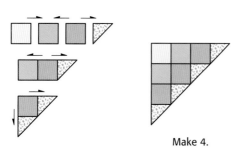

Make 4.

3 Sew a large pieced setting triangle from step 2 to
2 opposite sides of the appliqué section and press
the seams. Join the 2 remaining pieced triangles
to the other sides of the appliqué and press.

4 Join an F triangle to the 2 adjacent lower edges of
the 2 remaining appliqué blocks, as shown. In the
same manner, join F triangles to the 2 short sides
of the appliquéd triangles. Join these sections to
the opposite sides of the center unit.

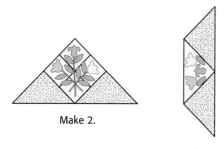

Make 2.

Make 2.

5 Referring to the quilt assembly diagram opposite,
join the appliqué block sections to the top and
bottom of the center unit and the appliqué
triangle sections to the sides of the quilt top.

6 To make the Pinwheel block corners, join 3
E triangles with a lavender, green, and light blue
Pinwheel block, as shown. Repeat to make 4
corner units. Attach 1 unit to each corner of the
center unit. Press the seams toward the center.

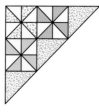

Make 4.

BORDERS

1 Join the 3 borders before adding them to the quilt
top. Make 4 sets each with a pink inner, lavender
middle, and green outer border sewn side by side.
Use the 6"-wide large-scale floral green print
strips, the 2½"-wide lavender print strips, and the
1½"-wide pink print strips. Press all seams toward
the green border.

2 Measure the width of the quilt top through the
center and trim the 2 shorter border sets to this
measurement. Sew these to the top and bottom of
the quilt top with the pink strips nearest the
center; press the seams toward the borders.

3 Measure the length of the quilt top through the
center and trim the 2 remaining border sets to
this measurement. Join a light blue Pinwheel

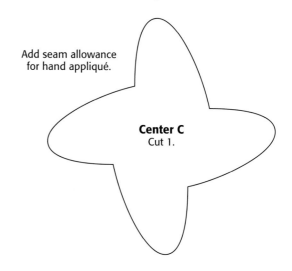

Add seam allowance
for hand appliqué.

Center C
Cut 1.

block to each end of the border sets and then join the borders to the sides of the quilt top in the same manner as the top and bottom borders.

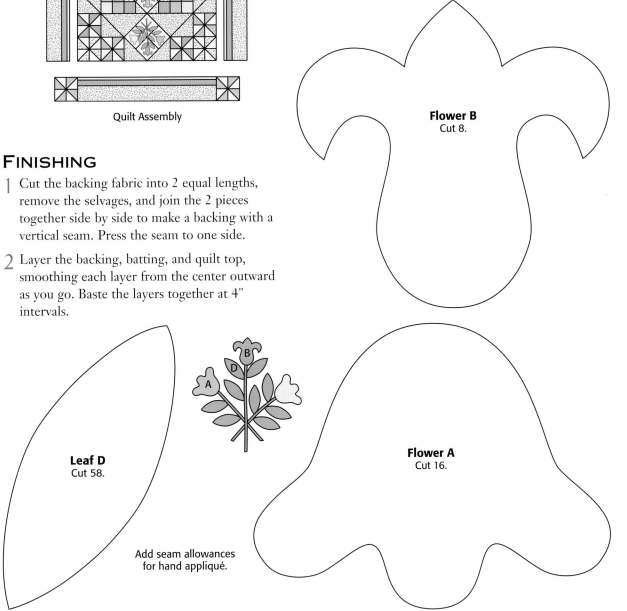

Quilt Assembly

FINISHING

1 Cut the backing fabric into 2 equal lengths, remove the selvages, and join the 2 pieces together side by side to make a backing with a vertical seam. Press the seam to one side.

2 Layer the backing, batting, and quilt top, smoothing each layer from the center outward as you go. Baste the layers together at 4" intervals.

3 Hand or machine quilt as desired. Becky's quilt was machine quilted with small stippling around the appliqué sections and a larger meandering pattern over the rest of the quilt.

4 Remove the basting and trim the edges of the quilt, leaving ¼" of batting and backing beyond the pieced quilt top to fill the binding. Join the 3"-wide lavender binding strips end to end; press the seams open. Attach the binding to the quilt, referring to "Binding" on page 94 for more details.

5 Label your quilt, including your name, the date, and any other relevant information.

Flower B
Cut 8.

Leaf D
Cut 58.

Add seam allowances for hand appliqué.

Flower A
Cut 16.

PANEL PATCH

Susan Murphy has captured an air of old-world charm with this lovely scrap quilt made in a selection of reproduction prints. Inspiration comes from many sources, and the design for this quilt began when Susan saw a picture of preprinted yardage from the 1850s. She found it impossible to move on to any other work until she had designed this quilt. Whether you work with reproduction prints as Susan did or randomly choose fabrics from your scrap bag, this quilt will be a delight to make.

To really mix things up, try using some of your lighter prints in the dark positions. Sometimes they can stand out as a dark print when placed next to one that is even lighter. Blurring the lines between light and dark a bit will give you a broader range of color and fabric combinations.

MATERIALS

Yardages are based on 42"-wide (107 cm) fabric.

- ¼ yd. (20 cm) *each* of 15 dark prints
- ¼ yd. (20 cm) *each* of 10 light prints
- ½ yd. (50 cm) of dark print for binding
- 2⅞ yds. (2.6 m) of backing fabric
- 51" x 67" (130 cm x 170 cm) piece of batting

Machine pieced and quilted by Susan Murphy.

Finished Block Size: 4" x 4" (10 cm square)
Finished Quilt Size: 45" x 61" (115 cm x 155 cm)

CUTTING

All cutting dimensions include ¼" seam allowances. Instructions are for cutting strips across the fabric width except where noted.

From the light prints, cut:
◆ 41 squares, 6½" x 6½"
◆ 166 rectangles, 1½" x 2½"

From the dark prints, cut:
◆ 41 squares, 6½" x 6½"
◆ 83 squares, 2½" x 2½"
◆ 166 rectangles, 1½" x 4½"

From the binding fabric, cut:
◆ 7 strips, 2½" x 42"

HOURGLASS BLOCK ASSEMBLY

1 Draw a diagonal line from corner to corner on the wrong side of the 6½" light squares. Place each light square right sides together with a 6½" dark square, and stitch ¼" away from each side of the drawn line. Cut the squares apart on the drawn line and press the resulting triangle squares open, pressing the seams toward the dark prints. Make a total of 82 triangle squares.

Make 82.

2 Draw a diagonal line on the wrong side of 41 of the triangle units; the line should run from the light to the dark corner, as shown. Pair the marked triangle squares with the 41 unmarked ones, ensuring that a dark triangle lies above a light triangle underneath, and vice versa. Be sure to mix the fabrics and colors as much as possible when pairing up the squares. Take care that the seams are butted snugly against one another at the center.

Stitch ¼" away from either side of the drawn line, and then cut along the drawn lines and press open the Hourglass blocks. Make 82 blocks.

Make 82.

3 Trim the blocks to a perfect 4½" square; a generous seam allowance has been included so that you can adjust the corners of your square ruler to fit perfectly on the diagonal lines of the pieced block.

COURTHOUSE STEPS BLOCK ASSEMBLY

1 Stitch the 1½" x 2½" light rectangles to opposite sides of the 2½" dark squares. Press the seams outward.

2 Stitch the 1½" x 4½" dark rectangles to the top and bottom of the square and press the seams outward to complete the Courthouse Steps blocks. Each block should measure 4½" square. Make 83 blocks.

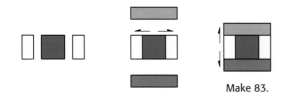

Make 83.

QUILT ASSEMBLY

1 Arrange the blocks in 15 horizontal rows of 11 blocks each, referring to the quilt photograph, opposite. Be sure to alternate the Courthouse Steps and Hourglass blocks as shown.

2 Rearrange the blocks as necessary to ensure an even distribution of the different fabrics and colors throughout the quilt. When you are satisfied with the placement, join the blocks together into rows, pressing the seams of each row in alternate directions.

3 Join the rows together to complete the quilt top; press carefully. Since no borders will be added, try not to stretch the edges of the patchwork out of shape. You may find it helpful to stay stitch by machine around the perimeter of the quilt about ¼" from the edge to prevent stretching.

FINISHING

1 Cut the backing fabric into 2 equal lengths, remove the selvages, and join the 2 pieces together side by side to make a backing with a horizontal seam. Press the seam to one side.

2 Layer the backing, batting, and quilt top, smoothing each layer from the center outward as you go. Baste the layers together at 4" intervals.

3 Hand or machine quilt as desired. Susan machine quilted in the ditch along the diagonal lines of the Hourglass blocks.

4 Remove the basting and trim the edges of the quilt, leaving ¼" of batting and backing beyond the pieced quilt top to fill the binding. Join the 2½"-wide binding strips end to end; press the seams open. Attach the binding to the quilt, referring to "Binding" on page 94 for more details.

5 Label your quilt, including your name, the date, and any other relevant information.

CHRISTMAS CRACKER

Jacky Hens provided her friends in the Cotton Reel Quilters with a pattern, green fabric, and an unusual black, red, and green fabric. Her friends supplied assorted red and cream fabrics and each made a block for Jacky. They presented the blocks to her as a birthday gift. In turn, Jacky assembled the blocks into a beautiful Christmas quilt.

As Jacky anticipated, when she pieced the blocks together without sashes, the corners created a lovely secondary pattern. What a wonderful gift this quilt would make for a special friend, or perhaps as a little holiday indulgence for yourself!

MATERIALS

Yardages are based on 42"-wide (107 cm) fabric.

- 1⅝ yds. (1.5 m) of feature print for blocks and borders

- 1⅝ yds. (1.5 m) of green print for blocks, borders, and binding

- 12 fat eighths of assorted red tone-on-tone prints for blocks

- 12 fat eighths of assorted cream tone-on-tone prints for background

- 1 yd. (90 cm) of cream tone-on-tone print for borders

- 3 yds. (2.7 m) of backing fabric

- 55" x 67" (140 cm x 170 cm) piece of batting

*Pieced by Jacky Hens and her quilt group,
the Cotton Reel Quilters. Machine quilted by Jacky Hens.*

Finished Block Size: 12" x 12" (30.5 cm square)
Finished Quilt Size: 48½" x 60½" (123 cm x 154 cm)

CUTTING

All cutting dimensions include ¼" seam allowances.
Instructions are for cutting strips across the fabric
width except where noted.

From *each* of the 12 red tone-on-tone prints, cut:

◆ 2 squares, 5¼" x 5¼"; cut each square twice
diagonally to yield 8 triangles (96 total)

◆ 1 square, 4½" x 4½" (12 total)

From *each* of the 12 cream tone-on-tone prints, cut:

◆ 1 square, 5¼" x 5¼"; cut each square twice
diagonally to yield 4 triangles (48 total)

◆ 4 squares, 2⅞" x 2⅞"; cut each square once
diagonally to yield 8 triangles (96 total)

◆ 4 squares, 2½" x 2½" (48 total)

From the feature print, cut:

◆ 2 strips, 5¼" x 42"; crosscut into 12 squares,
5¼" x 5¼". Cut each square twice diagonally to
yield 48 triangles.

◆ 2 strips, 2⅞" x 42"; crosscut into 24 squares,
2⅞" x 2⅞". Cut each square once diagonally
to yield 48 triangles

◆ 2 strips, 2½" x 42"; crosscut into 28 squares,
2½" x 2½"

◆ 7 strips, 4½" x 42"; crosscut into 50 squares,
4½" x 4½"

From the green print, cut:

◆ 6 strips, 2⅞" x 42"; crosscut into 72 squares,
2⅞" x 2⅞". Cut each square once diagonally to
yield 144 triangles.

◆ 7 strips, 2½" x 42"; crosscut into 104 squares,
2½" x 2½"

◆ 6 strips, 2½" x 42"

From the cream yardage, cut:

◆ 11 strips, 2½" x 42". From these strips, crosscut:

  ◆ 14 rectangles, 2½" x 12½"

  ◆ 92 squares, 2½" x 2½"

◆ 2 squares, 2⅞" x 2⅞"; cut each square once
diagonally to yield 4 triangles

BLOCK ASSEMBLY

While a dozen background and a dozen red fabrics
are used in this quilt to give it some added appeal,
the same cream and the same red fabrics are used
consistently throughout a single block. To help you
keep organized, the directions are for piecing one
block at a time.

1 Using red, cream, and feature-print 5¼" triangles,
join the cream and red triangles, sewing each pair
along the short side with the red fabric on top as
you sew, as shown. In the same manner, join the

feature-print triangles with the remaining red triangles, again sewing with the red triangles on top. Press all seams toward the red triangles.

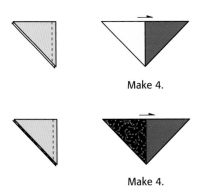

Make 4.

Make 4.

2 Join the red-and-cream units with the red-and-feature-print units to make 4 pieced squares for the red star points.

Star-Point Unit
Make 4.

3 For each corner unit, join 2 cream and 2 green 2⅞" triangles to make 2 triangle squares. Press the seams toward the green fabric. In the same manner, sew a green triangle to a feature print triangle. Referring to the diagram for placement, join the 3 triangle squares and a 2½" cream square together. Repeat to make a total of 4 identical corner units.

Corner Unit
Make 4.

4 Lay out the 4 red star-point units, the 4 corner units, and a 4½" red square for your block. Sew the components together in rows; then sew the rows together to complete the block.

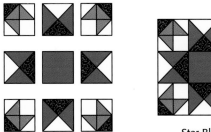

Star Block

5 Repeat steps 1–4 to complete 12 blocks.

QUILT ASSEMBLY

1 Arrange the blocks in 4 rows of 3 blocks each. Join the blocks together into rows, pressing the seams of each row in alternate directions.

2 Sew the rows together, paying particular attention when matching the points and the seam intersections.

BORDERS

This quilt has an inner and an outer border; both are pieced. The inner-border piecing completes the design while the outer border nicely frames it.

Inner Border

1 Lay a 2½" feature-print square on top of each end of a 2½" x 12½" cream rectangle with right sides together. Stitch diagonally across each square, as shown on page 82. Note that the diagonal slants in a different direction on either end of the rectangle. Press the feature print to the corner, making sure the corners match. To reduce bulk,

trim the inner feature triangle ¼" away from the stitching line. Make 14 of these inner-border rectangle units.

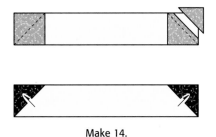

Make 14.

2 Make 4 triangle squares by joining 2⅞" cream triangles and 2⅞" feature-print triangles.

3 Join 4 border rectangles together end to end with the triangles positioned so that they form a larger triangle when joined. Make a second identical border. Referring to the quilt photograph on page 80, stitch these borders to the opposite sides of the quilt top.

Side Border
Make 2.

4 Make the borders for the top and bottom of the quilt in the same manner, but this time join only 3 rectangles per border. Add a triangle square to each end of these borders, making sure the feature-print triangles adjoin those on the ends of the border. Stitch the borders to the quilt top, again matching seam intersections.

Top or Bottom Border
Make 2.

Outer Border

1 Place a 2½" green square right sides together and with the corners aligned on top of a 4½" feature-print square. Stitch diagonally across the green square. Fold the corner open, making sure it aligns exactly with the square underneath, and then trim the inner triangle of the green fabric to reduce bulk. Place another green square on the adjacent corner as shown and stitch; trim and press it as before.

2 Stitch a 2½" cream square to each of the 2 remaining corners in the same manner. Use a ruler to make sure the square measures 4½" and square it up with your rotary cutter if necessary.

Make 46.

3 Repeat to make a total of 46 pieced squares.

4 To make the 4 corner units, place a 2½" green square over 3 of the corners on each of the 4 remaining 4½" feature-print squares. Stitch diagonally across each green square as before. Flip the corners over and trim the inner triangle to reduce bulk. Press and trim the units to 4½" square.

Make 4.

5 Make 2 borders of 13 pieced squares each, making sure the cream triangles are all on the same side of the borders. Attach the borders to opposite sides of the quilt top, matching the points of the feature-print squares and ensuring that the green print is positioned along the outer edge.

6 Make 2 borders of 10 pieced squares each. Stitch a corner unit to each end of the borders and attach the borders to the top and bottom of the quilt top, matching the points of the feature squares and ensuring the green print is at the outer edge.

FINISHING

1 Cut the backing fabric into 2 equal lengths, remove the selvages, and join the 2 pieces side by side to make a backing with a vertical seam. Press the seam to one side.

2 Layer the backing, batting, and quilt top, smoothing each layer from the center outward as you go. Baste the layers together at 4" intervals.

3 Hand or machine quilt as desired. Jacky machine quilted her quilt mostly in the ditch and with an on-point square quilted in the red center square of each block.

4 Remove the basting and trim the edges of the quilt, leaving ¼" of batting and backing beyond the pieced quilt top to fill the binding. Join the 2½"-wide binding strips end to end; press the seams open. Attach the binding to the quilt, referring to "Binding" on page 94 for more details.

5 Label your quilt, including your name, the date, and any other relevant information.

SCRAPPY GRETCHEN

Kerrilyn Gavin's scrap quilt made of Gretchen blocks is simply a delight, creating a real sense of diagonal movement and displaying a beautiful show of color.

"It's simpler than it looks," says Canberra quiltmaker Kerrilyn of the Gretchen block. That's because to avoid the tedious tracing of shapes around templates, Kerrilyn adapted the pattern to include nothing but right triangles— a shape easily cut with a rotary cutter. She simply trimmed off the unneeded corners for a quick and easy piecing technique with excellent results.

This quilt is ideal for using up all of those scraps you can't bear to throw away. Just sort your scraps into one dark pile and one light pile; as long as you use a very light fabric for your background, you can't go wrong. Simply cut and stitch and watch those fabrics disappear from the scrap bag to a new home on the bed.

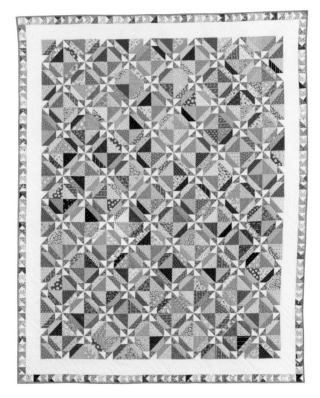

Pieced and quilted by Kerrilyn Gavin.

Finished Block Size: 12" x 12" (30 cm square)
Finished Quilt Size: 78½" x 96½" (199 cm x 245 cm)

MATERIALS

Yardages are based on 42"-wide (107 cm) fabric.

◆ 4 yds. (3.7 m) *total* of a large selection of dark print scraps (minimum size 5" or 12.5 cm square) for blocks and pieced border

◆ 4 yds. (3.7 m) *total* of a large selection of medium print scraps (minimum size 5" or 12.5 cm square) for blocks and pieced border

◆ 2½ yds. (2.3 m) of light print or solid for block background and inner border

◆ 1 yd. (90 cm) of red print for pinwheels

◆ ⅞ yd. (70 cm) of dark check for binding

◆ 5¾ yds. (5.3 m) of backing fabric

◆ 87" x 102" (220 cm x 260 cm) piece of batting

CUTTING

All cutting dimensions include ¼" seam allowances. Instructions are for cutting strips across the fabric width except where noted.

From the dark prints, cut:

◆ 154 squares, 4⅞" x 4⅞"; cut each square once diagonally to yield 308 triangles

◆ 43 squares, 2¼" x 2¼"; cut each square once diagonally to yield 86 triangles

◆ 43 squares, 2⅞" x 2⅞"; cut each square once diagonally to yield 86 triangles

From the medium prints, cut:

◆ 154 squares, 4⅞" x 4⅞"; cut each square once diagonally to yield 308 triangles

◆ 42 squares, 2¼" x 2¼"; cut each square once diagonally to yield 84 triangles

◆ 42 squares, 2⅞" x 2⅞"; cut each square once diagonally to yield 84 triangles

From the light fabric, cut on the lengthwise grain:

◆ 2 strips, 4½" x 84½"

◆ 2 strips, 4½" x 74½"

From the remaining light fabric, cut:

◆ 21 strips, 2⅞" x 42"; crosscut into 154 squares, 2⅞" x 2⅞". Cut each square once diagonally to yield 308 triangles.

◆ 5 strips, 4⅛" x 42"; crosscut into 43 squares, 4⅛" x 4⅛". Cut each square twice diagonally to yield 172 triangles. (You'll have 2 extra.)

From the red print, cut:

◆ 12 strips, 2⅞" x 42"; crosscut into 154 squares, 2⅞" x 2⅞". Cut each square once diagonally to yield 308 triangles.

From the dark check fabric, cut:

◆ 2½"-wide bias strips, enough to yield 360" of length

BLOCK ASSEMBLY

The quilt shown is made of 35 blocks and 7 half blocks. The blocks are composed of 4 quadrants; half blocks use only 2 quadrants.

1 Join the 4⅞" dark print triangles right sides together with the 4⅞" medium print triangles. Press the seams toward the dark triangles. Make 308 triangle squares. Divide the triangle squares into 2 piles of 154 each.

Make 308.

2 Stitch a 2⅞" light print triangle to each side of half of the dark triangles as shown, and press the seams toward the dark triangles.

Stitch the 2⅞" red print triangles to each side of half of the medium print triangles and press the seams toward the red triangles.

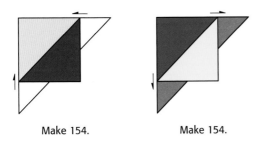

Make 154.   Make 154.

3 Align your rotary-cutting ruler along the long edges of the small triangles, while at the same time aligning the 45° line on your ruler with the short edge of the large triangle. Then trim the protruding corner of the large triangle, as shown. Repeat for all 308 units.

Trim.

4 Join a unit with light triangles to a unit with red triangles along the diagonal to complete a quarter block.

Quarter Block.
Make 154.

5 When all quarter blocks have been assembled, join them together into complete blocks and half blocks. Be sure to stitch them together as shown so the rotation of the red and white triangles will always be the same. Otherwise, the pinwheels won't be formed in your completed quilt.

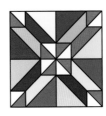

Full Block   Half Block

QUILT ASSEMBLY

1 Referring to the quilt photograph, opposite, arrange the blocks in 7 rows of 5 blocks each. Then add a half block to the end of each horizontal row. Be sure to step back and check your layout for a good mix of colors throughout the quilt top.

2 When you are satisfied with the block arrangement, join the blocks together into rows. Press the seams of alternate rows in opposite directions.

3 Stitch the rows together, matching the seam intersections. Press the quilt top.

BORDERS

A pieced border is set off by a plain inner border. Using an inner border also makes it easier to fit the outer border as it can be trimmed for a perfect fit without jeopardizing any of the block piecing.

Inner Border

Stitch the 4½" x 74½" light border strips to opposite sides of the quilt top and press the seams outward. Join the 2 remaining border strips to the top and bottom of the quilt top and press the seams outward.

Outer Border

1 Stitch a 4⅛" light triangle to a 4⅛" print triangle along the short side, with the light triangle on top. All of the light triangles, sewn in this manner, will form a line of "arrows" in the finished border. Press the seams toward the print triangles. Repeat with the remaining triangles to make 170 triangle units.

Make 170.

2 Join each triangle unit from step 1 to a 2⅞" print triangle to form a square.

3 Stitch the pieced squares together to make 2 borders containing 37 pieced squares, ensuring the squares are rotated so that the light triangle is always positioned on the right side of the square.

Stitch these borders to the top and bottom of the quilt top, with the light background triangles pointing clockwise around the quilt. Press the seams toward the pieced border to prevent show-through on the light border.

4 Stitch the remaining pieced squares together to make 2 borders of 48 squares each. Join these borders to opposite sides of the quilt top. Again, press the seams toward the pieced border.

FINISHING

1 Cut the backing fabric into 2 equal lengths, remove the selvages, and join the 2 pieces side by side to make a backing with a vertical seam. Press the seam to one side.

2 Layer the backing, batting, and quilt top, smoothing each layer from the center outward as you go. Baste the layers together at 4" intervals.

3 Hand or machine quilt as desired. Kerrilyn's quilt is quilted in the ditch along the diagonal edges of the larger triangles, and these quilting lines are carried through into the borders.

4 Remove the basting and trim the edges of the quilt, leaving ¼" of batting and backing beyond the pieced quilt top to fill the binding. Join the 2½"-wide binding strips end to end; press the seams open. Attach the binding to the quilt, referring to "Binding" on page 94 for more details.

5 Label your quilt, including your name, the date, and any other relevant information.

QUILTMAKING BASICS

*Whether you're new to quiltmaking or you're simply ready to learn a new technique,
you'll find this quiltmaking basics section filled with helpful information
that can make putting your quilt together a pleasurable experience.*

FABRICS AND SUPPLIES

Fabrics: Select high-quality, 100% cotton fabrics. They hold their shape well and are easy to handle. Regarding fabric measurements, the term *fat quarter* refers to 18" x 20" (45 x 50 cm) and *fat eighth* refers to 9" x 20" (25 x 50 cm) fabric.

Marking tools: Various tools are available to mark fabric when tracing around templates or marking quilting designs. Use a sharp No. 2 pencil or a fine-lead mechanical pencil on lighter-colored fabrics, and use a silver or chalk pencil on darker fabrics. Be sure to test your marking tool to make sure you can remove the marks easily.

Needles: A size 10/70 or 12/80 works well for machine piecing most cottons. A larger size needle, such as a 14/90, works best for machine quilting. For hand appliqué, choose a needle that will glide easily through the edges of the appliqué pieces. Size 10 (fine) to size 12 (very fine) needles work well. For hand quilting, use Betweens, which are short, very sharp needles made specifically for this purpose.

Pins: Long, fine silk pins slip easily through fabric, making them perfect for patchwork.

Rotary-cutting tools: You will need a rotary cutter, a cutting mat, and a clear acrylic ruler. Rotary-cutting rulers are available in a variety of sizes; some of the most frequently used sizes include 6" x 6", 6" x 24", 12" x 12", and 15" x 15".

Scissors: Use your best scissors only for cutting fabric. Use craft scissors to cut paper, cardboard, and template plastic. Sharp embroidery scissors or thread snips are handy for clipping threads.

Seam ripper: Use this tool to remove stitches from incorrectly sewn seams.

Sewing machine: To machine piece, you'll need a sewing machine that has a good straight stitch. You'll also need a walking foot or darning foot if you plan to machine quilt.

Template plastic: Use clear or frosted plastic (available at quilt shops) to make durable, accurate templates.

Thread: Use a good-quality, all-purpose cotton or cotton-covered polyester thread for piecing.

ROTARY CUTTING

Instructions for quick, easy rotary cutting are provided wherever possible. All measurements include standard ¼"-wide seam allowances. If you are unfamiliar with rotary cutting, read the brief introduction below. For more detailed information, see *Shortcuts: A Concise Guide to Rotary Cutting* by Donna Lynn Thomas (Martingale & Company, 1999).

1 To cut squares, cut strips in the required widths. Trim the selvage ends of the strips. Align the left edge of the strips with the correct ruler markings.

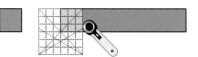

2 To make a half-square triangle, begin by cutting a square ⅞" larger than the desired finished size of the short side of the triangle. Then cut the square once diagonally, corner to corner. The short sides of each triangle are on the straight grain of the fabric.

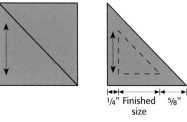

¼" Finished   ⅝"
size

¼" + ⅝" = ⅞"

3 To make a quarter-square triangle, begin by cutting a square 1¼" larger than the desired finished size of the long edge of the triangle. Then cut the square twice diagonally, corner to corner. The long side of each triangle is on the straight grain of the fabric.

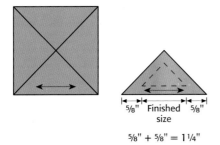

⅝"   Finished   ⅝"
size

⅝" + ⅝" = 1¼"

MACHINE PIECING

Most blocks in this book are designed for easy rotary cutting and quick piecing. Some blocks, however, require the use of templates for particular shapes, such as "Pie Quilt" on page 35. Templates for machine piecing include the required ¼"-wide seam allowances.

You need to maintain a consistent ¼"-wide seam allowance. Otherwise, the quilt blocks will not be the desired finished size. If that happens, the size of everything else in the quilt is affected, including alternate blocks, sashings, and borders.

Some machines have a special patchwork foot that measures exactly ¼" from the center needle position to the edge of the foot, enabling you to use the edge of the presser foot to guide the fabric for a perfect ¼"-wide seam allowance. If your machine doesn't have such a foot, create a seam guide by placing the edge of a piece of tape, moleskin, or a magnetic seam guide ¼" away from the needle.

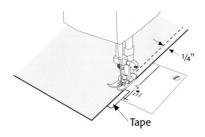

¼"

Tape

PRESSING

The traditional rule in quiltmaking is to press seams to one side, toward the darker color wherever possible. First press the seams flat from the wrong side of the fabric; then press the seams in the desired direction from the right side. Press carefully to avoid distorting the shapes.

When joining two seamed units, plan ahead and press the seam allowances in opposite directions, as shown. This reduces bulk and makes it easier to match the seam lines. The seam allowances will butt against each other where two seams meet, making it easier to sew units with perfectly matched seam intersections.

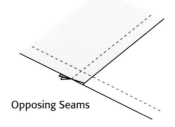

Opposing Seams

MAKING APPLIQUÉ TEMPLATES

Place template plastic over each pattern piece and trace with a fine-line permanent marker. Do not add seam allowances. Cut out the templates on the drawn lines. You need only one template for each different motif or shape. Write the pattern name and grain-line arrow (if applicable) on the template.

FREEZER-PAPER APPLIQUÉ

Freezer paper, which is coated on one side, is often used to help make perfectly shaped appliqués.

1 Trace around the plastic template on the uncoated side of the freezer paper with a sharp pencil.

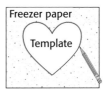

Freezer paper

Template

2 Cut out the traced design on the pencil line. Do not add seam allowances.

3 With the shiny side of the paper against the wrong side of your appliqué fabric, iron the freezer-paper cutout in place with a hot, dry iron.

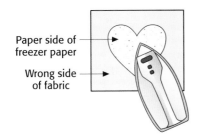

Paper side of freezer paper →

Wrong side of fabric →

4 Cut out the fabric shape, adding ¼" seam allowances all around the outside edge of the freezer paper.

5 Turn and baste the seam allowance over the freezer-paper edges by hand, or use a fabric glue stick. Clip inside points and fold outside points.

Clip point.

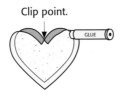

GLUE

6 Pin or baste the design to the background fabric or block. Appliqué the design using the traditional appliqué stitch described at right.

7 Remove any basting stitches. Cut a small slit in the background fabric behind the appliqué and remove the freezer paper with tweezers. If you used glue stick, soak the piece in warm water for a few minutes before removing the freezer paper.

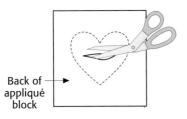

Back of appliqué block →

TRADITIONAL APPLIQUÉ STITCH

The traditional appliqué stitch or blind stitch is appropriate for sewing all appliqué shapes, including sharp points and curves.

1 Thread the needle with an approximately 18" single strand of thread in a color that closely matches the color of your appliqué. Knot the thread tail.

2 Hide the knot by slipping the needle into the seam allowance from the wrong side of the appliqué piece, bringing it out on the fold line.

3 Work from right to left if you are right-handed, or from left to right if you are left-handed.

4 To make the first stitch, insert the needle into the background right next to where the needle came out of the appliqué fabric. Bring the needle up through the edge of the appliqué, about ⅛" away from the first stitch.

5 As you bring the needle up, pierce the basted edge of the appliqué piece, catching only 1 or 2 threads of the edge.

6 Again, take a stitch into the background block right next to where the thread came up through the appliqué. Bring the needle up about ⅛" away from the previous stitch, again catching the basted edge of the appliqué.

7 Give the thread a slight tug and continue stitching.

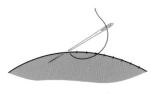

Appliqué Stitch

Note: The stitches in these appliqué illustrations are shown large to indicate placement. The stitches should not show in the completed work.

8 To end your stitching, pull the needle through to the wrong side of the background fabric. Behind the appliqué piece, take 2 small stitches, making knots by taking your needle through the loops. Check the right side to see if the thread shows through the background. If it does, take one more small stitch on the back side to direct the tail of the thread under the appliqué fabric.

91

FUSIBLE APPLIQUÉ

Using fusible web is a fast and fun way to appliqué. If the appliqué pattern is directional, you need to make a reverse tracing of the pattern so the pattern will match the original design when fused in place. Otherwise, your finished project will be the reverse of the project shown in the book. You don't need to make reverse tracings for patterns that are symmetrical or for ones that are already printed in reverse.

Refer to the manufacturer's directions when applying fusible web to your fabrics; each brand is a little different, and pressing for too long may result in fusible web that doesn't stick well.

1 Trace or draw your shape on the paper backing side of the fusible web. Cut out the shape, leaving about a ¼" margin all around the outline.

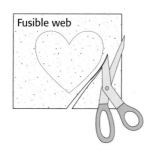

2 Fuse shapes to the wrong side of your fabric.

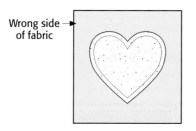

3 Cut out the shape exactly on the marked line. Remove the paper backing, position the shape on the background, and press it in place with your iron.

MAKING BIAS TUBES FOR APPLIQUÉ

Bias tubes—often used for appliquéd stems and basket handles—are easy to make with the help of metal or nylon bias press bars. These handy notions come in sets of assorted widths. Most projects in this book use the ½" size.

1 Cut a piece of fabric as instructed in the specific quilt instructions. Cut the fabric into 1¼"-wide bias strips using a rotary cutter and ruler.

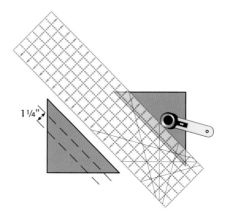

2 Fold each strip in half lengthwise, wrong sides together. Stitch ½" from the folded edge. This will leave a ⅛" seam allowance.

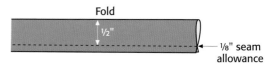

3 Insert a ½" bias bar, roll the seam so it is centered along one flat edge of the bias bar, and press flat. Remove the bias bar. The finished strip will measure ½" wide.

SQUARING UP BLOCKS

When your blocks are complete, take the time to square them up. Use a large square ruler to measure your blocks and make sure they are the desired size plus an exact ¼" on each side for seam allowances. For example, if you are making 9" blocks, they

92

should all measure 9½" before you sew them together. Trim the larger blocks to match the size of the smallest one. Be sure to trim all four sides; otherwise your block will be lopsided.

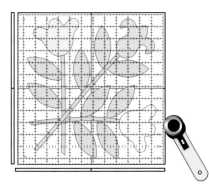

If your blocks are not the required finished size, adjust all the other components of the quilt, such as sashing and borders, accordingly.

Preparing to Quilt

If you'll be quilting your project by hand or on your home sewing machine, you'll want to refer to the following directions below for marking, layering, basting, and quilting. However, if you plan to have a professional machine quilter quilt your project, check with that person first. Quilts do not need to be layered and basted for long-arm machine quilting, nor do they usually need to be marked.

Marking the Quilting Lines

Marking is not necessary if you plan to quilt in the ditch (along the seam lines) or outline quilt a uniform distance from seam lines. For more complex quilting designs, however, mark the quilt top before the quilt is layered with batting and backing.

Choose a marking tool that will be visible on your fabric and test it on fabric scraps to be sure the marks can be removed easily. See "Marking Tools" on page 89 for options. Masking tape can be used to mark straight quilting lines. Tape only small sections at a time and remove the tape when you stop at the end of the day, or the sticky residue may be difficult to remove from the fabric.

Layering and Basting the Quilt

The quilt "sandwich" consists of the backing, batting, and quilt top. The quilt backing and batting should be at least 4" larger than the quilt top all the

way around. For large quilts, it is usually necessary to sew two or three lengths of fabric together to make a backing that is large enough. Trim away the selvages before piecing the lengths together. Press the seams open to make quilting easier.

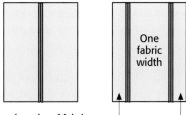

Two lengths of fabric seamed in the center | Partial fabric width

Batting comes packaged in standard bed sizes, or it can be purchased by the yard. Several weights or thicknesses are available. Thick battings are fine for tied quilts and comforters; a thinner batting is better, however, if you intend to quilt by hand or machine.

1 Spread the backing wrong side up on a flat, clean surface. Anchor it with pins or masking tape. Be careful not to stretch the backing out of shape.

2 Spread the batting over the backing, smoothing out any wrinkles.

3 Center the pressed quilt top on top of the batting. Smooth out any wrinkles and make sure the quilt-top edges are parallel to the edges of the backing.

4 Starting in the center, baste with needle and thread and work diagonally to each corner. Then baste a grid of horizontal and vertical lines 6" to 8" apart. Finish by basting around the edges.

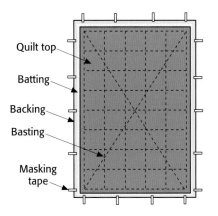

For machine quilting, baste the layers with #2 rustproof safety pins. Place pins about 6" to 8" apart, away from the areas you intend to quilt.

QUILTING TECHNIQUES

Some of the projects in this book were hand quilted, others were machine quilted, and some were quilted on long-arm quilting machines. The choice is yours!

Hand Quilting

To quilt by hand, you will need short, sturdy needles (called Betweens), quilting thread, and a thimble to fit the middle finger of your sewing hand. Most quilters also use a frame or hoop to support their work. Use the smallest needle you can comfortably handle; the finer the needle, the smaller your stitches will be. The basics of hand quilting are explained below. For more information on hand quilting, refer to *Loving Stitches: A Guide to Fine Hand Quilting* by Jeana Kimball (That Patchwork Place, 1992).

1 Thread your needle with a single strand of quilting thread about 18" long. Make a small knot and insert the needle in the top layer about 1" from the place where you want to start stitching. Pull the needle out at the point where quilting will begin and gently pull the thread until the knot pops through the fabric and into the batting.

2 Take small, evenly spaced stitches through all 3 quilt layers. Rock the needle up and down through all layers until you have 3 or 4 stitches on the needle. Place your other hand underneath the quilt so you can feel the needle point with the tip of your finger when a stitch is taken.

3 To end a line of quilting, make a small knot close to the last stitch; then backstitch, running the thread a needle's length through the batting. Gently pull the thread until the knot pops into the batting; clip the thread at the quilt's surface.

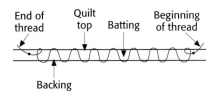

Machine Quilting

For straight-line quilting, it is extremely helpful to have a walking foot to help feed the quilt layers through the machine without shifting or puckering. Some machines have a built-in walking foot; other machines require a separate attachment.

For free-motion quilting, you need a darning foot and the ability to drop or cover the feed dogs on your machine. With free-motion quilting, you guide the fabric in the direction of the design rather than turning the fabric under the needle. Use free-motion quilting to outline quilt a fabric motif or to create stippling or other curved designs.

Long-Arm Machine Quilting

If you prefer to have your quilt quilted by a professional, ask at your local quilt shop for references about someone in your area who does this type of work. Generally, for long-arm machine quilting, you don't layer and baste the quilt prior to giving it to the quilter, nor do you have to mark the quilting designs. Check with your quilter to be sure of specifications regarding batting and backing sizes before cutting or piecing yours.

FINISHING

Bind your quilt, add a hanging sleeve if one is needed, and label your quilt, and you're finished.

Binding

For a French double-fold binding, cut strips 2" to 2½" wide across the width of the fabric. (Some quilters prefer narrow binding, especially if a low-loft batting is used. If you're using a thicker batting, you may want to use 2½" strips.) You will need enough strips to go around the perimeter of the quilt, plus 10" for seams and to turn the corners.

1 Sew the binding strips together to make 1 long strip. Join strips at right angles, right sides together, and stitch across the corner, as shown. Trim excess fabric and press the seams open.

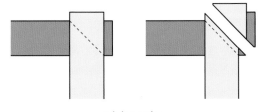

Joining Strips

2 Fold the strip in half lengthwise, wrong sides together, and press.

3 Trim the batting and backing even with the quilt top. If you plan to add a hanging sleeve, do so now before attaching the binding (see page 96).

4 Starting near the middle of one side of the quilt, align the raw edges of the binding with the raw edges of the quilt top. Using a walking foot and a ¼"-wide seam allowance, begin stitching the binding to the quilt leaving a 6" tail unstitched. Stop stitching ¼" away from the corner of the quilt.

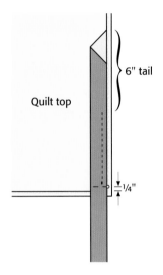

6" tail

Quilt top

¼"

5 Lift the needle out of the quilt; then turn the quilt so you will be stitching down the next side. Fold the binding up, away from the quilt, with raw edges aligned. Fold the binding back down onto

itself, even with the edge of the quilt top. Begin stitching ¼" from the corner, backstitching to secure the stitches. Repeat the process on the remaining edges and corners of the quilt.

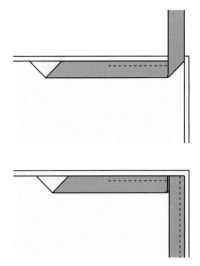

6 On the last side of the quilt, stop stitching about 7" from where you began. Overlap the ending binding tail with the starting tail. Trim the binding ends with a perpendicular cut so the overlap is exactly the same distance as the cut width of your binding strips. (If your binding strips are 2½" wide, the overlap should be 2½"; for 2"-wide binding, the overlap should be 2".)

2½" overlap

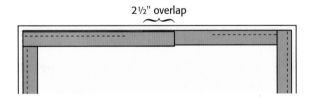

7 Open up the 2 ends of folded binding. Place the tails right sides together so they join to form a right angle, as shown. Pin the binding tails together; then mark a diagonal stitching line from corner to corner.

Pin ends together.
Draw diagonal line.

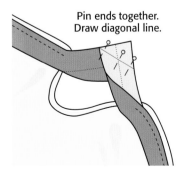

8 Stitch the binding tails together on the marked line. Trim the seam allowance to ¼"; press the seam open to reduce bulk. Refold the binding, align the edges with the raw edges of the quilt top, and finish sewing it in place.

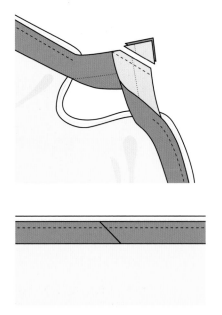

9 Fold the binding to the back of the quilt top to cover the machine-stitching line. Hand stitch in place, mitering the corners.

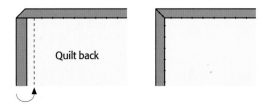

Quilt back

Adding a Hanging Sleeve

If you plan to display your finished quilt on the wall, be sure to add a hanging sleeve to hold the rod.

1 Using leftover fabric from the quilt backing, cut a strip 6" to 8" wide and 1" shorter than the width of your quilt. Fold the ends under ½", and then again ½" to make a hem. Stitch in place.

2 Fold the fabric strip in half lengthwise, wrong sides together, and baste the raw edges to the top of the quilt back. The top edge of the sleeve will be secured when the binding is attached.

3 Finish the sleeve after the binding has been attached by blindstitching the bottom of the sleeve in place. Push the bottom edge of the sleeve up just a bit to provide a little give so the hanging rod does not put strain on the quilt.

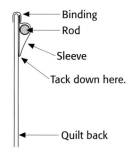

Signing Your Quilt

Future generations will be interested to know more than just who made a quilt and when, so be sure to include the name of the quilt, your name, your hometown, the date, the name of the recipient if the quilt is a gift, and any other interesting or important information about the quilt. The information can be handwritten, typed, or embroidered.